How to Mend a Br❤ken Heart

Letting Go and Moving On

Aleta Koman, M.Ed.

CB
CONTEMPORARY BOOKS

Library of Congress Cataloging-in-Publication Data

Koman, Aleta.
   How to mend a broken heart : letting go and moving on / Aleta
Koman.
      p.   cm.
   Includes bibliographical references and index.
   ISBN 0-8092-3172-7 (cloth); 0-8092-2949-8 (paper)
   1. Loss (Psychology)   2. Grief.   3. Adjustment (Psychology)
I. Title.
BF575.D35K66   1997
158' .2—dc20   96-41946
                                                          CIP

Interior design and production by Susan H. Hartman

Published by Contemporary Books
An imprint of NTC/Contemporary Publishing Company
4255 West Touhy Avenue, Lincolnwood (Chicago), Illinois 60646-1975 U.S.A.
Copyright © 1997 by Aleta Koman, M.Ed., and Edward Myers
Printed in the United States of America
International Standard Book Number 0-8092-3172-7 (cloth)
                                    0-8092-2949-8 (paper)
18   17   16   15   14   13   12   11   10   9   8   7   6   5   4   3   2   1

How to Mend a Broken Heart

▲ △ ▲

All case histories and examples mentioned in this book are composites of two or more persons. All personal names (except for those of the psychologists and other theorists I quote) have been changed. All potentially identifying details—professions, ages, places of residence, family backgrounds, etc.—have also been changed. All quotations (again, excepting those of psychologists and other theorists) are paraphrases with some details changed to protect identities. Any similarities between these examples and any actual persons, either living or deceased, are purely coincidental.

This book is not intended as a substitute for psychotherapy with a qualified professional.

▲ △ ▲

To all those who have suffered the pain and grief
of having their hearts broken
by someone they deeply loved.

And to my son, Jason,
who is the heart of my soul!

Contents

*P*reface

*H*ow to Mend a Broken Heart is a self-help book for people who are coping with a sense of loss following the end of a relationship. Unlike most books about loss and its emotional consequences, *How to Mend a Broken Heart* doesn't focus on the impact of loss following a death; rather, it concentrates on the difficulties that people feel after other kinds of losses. Among these losses are the following:

▲ loss of a partner through divorce
▲ loss of a heterosexual partner other than through divorce (separation, abandonment, etc.)
▲ loss of a homosexual partner
▲ loss of a sibling relationship
▲ loss of some other family relationship
▲ loss of a close friend
▲ loss of access to grandchildren through custody disputes
▲ loss of a job

What people experience in the aftermath of these losses is, of course, highly individual; since each relationship differs from every other relationship, each person's experience of loss will differ from what other people experience. At the same time, all losses share certain features even though their specifics are unique. Understanding the general nature of loss will help you understand the particular nature of your own experience.

I've written *How to Mend a Broken Heart* to help people come to terms with what they feel following a significant loss. As a counselor and teacher, I know that no magic wand exists that can take away the pain of brokenheartedness; I would never claim that this or any other book is a panacea. However, the knowledge of what happens following a loss—whether the loss occurs after a death, a divorce, a sibling rift, or some other event—can grant you the power to take control of your life again. *How to Mend a Broken Heart* is my effort to share the knowledge I've acquired over many years in my several professional roles.

How to Mend a Broken Heart has a four-part structure.

Part I, "Shattered Dreams and Broken Promises," explores the frustration, sadness, and pain that most people experience when the reality of their human ties falls short of fantasy. I say *fantasy* because, to some extent, all people base their relationships on imagined or projected assumptions—a legacy of personal and cultural images of what their emotional ties should be. Part I examines this legacy and delineates five common but damaging beliefs that produce it. All five of these beliefs hold sway over people. Regrettably, they can do great damage. The result is a heightened state of vulnerability when a relationship comes to an end.

Part II, "Real People, Real Problems," sketches ten relationships in which people struggle with the consequences of a broken heart. Some of these relationships are typical of the most common kinds of loss. Annette and Jack find that despite their best intentions, their marriage deteriorates. Wanda struggles with William, her abusive husband. Sandy and Jim experience the bittersweet aftermath of their first love affair. Other relationships are statistically less common but still humanly significant. Karen struggles with a major family rift. Jed and Nancy, who are brother and sister, cope with smoldering mutual resentments. Marissa and Julie deal with the collapse of their lesbian relationship. My intention throughout is to portray both the variety and the commonality of loss.

After showing the breadth and depth of loss, I proceed to Part III, "Mending a Broken Heart," which is a systematic program that most people can apply to their own personal experiences. This program involves six steps: (1) understanding the nature of loss, (2) focusing on the self, (3) dealing with the Shadow Side, (4) stabilizing your life, (5) becoming aware of your recovery, and (6) accepting progress, not perfection. Again, I need to emphasize that this program isn't a panacea for coping with loss. Thoughtfully considered, however, it can help you deal with the shock, sadness, and disorientation you feel after losing a significant relationship; and it can assist you in reevaluating your perceptions of yourself and moving on toward new vitality and enjoyment of life.

Finally, Part IV, "Resources," provides specific kinds of help to facilitate your process of recovery. Two appendices list helpful organizations and books that can help you mend your broken heart.

The overall principle throughout this book is that if you can understand the nature of loss and its effects, you can learn to deal better with emotional wounds that affect you now and that may continue to cause you pain. My purpose in writing *How to Mend a Broken Heart* is to help foster that understanding. I offer you my best wishes as you start to heal the wounds you have suffered and as you move toward the relationships you truly want.

$\mathcal{A}$cknowledgments

$\mathbf{M}$any people have made this book possible. I wish I could thank everyone individually, but an acknowledgments section allows me only to start thanking all the wonderfully supportive people in my life.

First, I would like to thank Edward Myers for his editorial expertise; Peter May, for introducing me to my agent, Faith Hamlin; and Faith herself, who has made this book possible. I would also like to gratefully acknowledge my editor, Susan Schwartz, for her interest and support throughout the course of this project.

I also wish to thank my son, Jason, for his support and enthusiasm for this project; Woody Umanoff for his support and insights; Susan Adelman for sharing her insights and wisdom; my parents, Morton and Rhoda, for their belief and support throughout my personal journey; my two grandmothers, Sarah Miller-Goldstein and Sylvia Greenberg-Levine, for having sustained me in many ways; my sister Abby and my brother-in-law, Russ; my sister Ivy; my brother, Stuart; my sister-in-law Brenda; and all the other members of my family for the roles they've played in my life.

Other kinds of assistance and support came from friends and colleagues. I'll list just a few for their special efforts. To Charlotte Umanoff, George Delany, Beth Kantrowitz-Scheindlin and Ben Scheindlin, Diane Buhl and Mark Polebaum, Melanie Freeman-Jordan and Bob Jordan, Suzanne Bates, Joyce Karlson, Doreen Reed, Maureen Tennis, Jody Snider, Steve Snyder, Paul Wagner, Josh Biswanger, Rachel Burg, Jason Rich, Gail and Ruven Liebhaber, Faina and Richard Smith, Jennifer and Matt Carmody, Linda and Jim Anear, Carol and Bob Galloway, Fernita Wynn, Emily Barsh, Stephen Hall, Dinno, Susan Foote, Cheryl Gatto, Tara Smith, Amy Boulter, and Cheryl Williams; also Jackie Ramos, Phil Amato, Jennifer Swanberg, Marjorie Bakken, Theresa Perry, Marcia Folsom, Patricia Hogan, Sue Swap, Muriel Hirt, Fran Littman, Linda Braun, Joan Bergstrom, Fran Perkins, Grace Pantano, Eleanor Nelson: thank you all for your input and for the special relationships we have formed over the years.

Last but certainly not least, my heartfelt thanks to all of my students, clients, and friends for the privilege of getting to know you over the years. I have been blessed to have known each and every one of you. You are each a living testament to the resiliency of the human spirit!

PART I

Shattered Dreams and Broken Promises

As a practicing psychotherapist, I see many people who are struggling with the aftermath of failed relationships. They are brokenhearted—angry, sad, confused, and depressed. They feel betrayed and abandoned, and they are often unsure how to proceed with their lives now that an important bond has been severed.

As an on-air specialist in family issues and relationships on several national television talk shows, I watch an even greater variety of people coping with loss after their marriages, love affairs, and other relationships have ended. They, too, are brokenhearted, and their numbers are vast.

▲ Herb lost his longtime job as a software engineer some months ago. To numb his pain and anxiety, Herb resorted to having an extramarital affair. His wife reacted furiously to Herb's infidelity and ended their eighteen-year marriage. Herb feels that his entire world is collapsing.

▲ Patrice, who was always extremely close to her mother, Anna, disapproves of Anna's recent remarriage. Patrice feels that her mother is so obsessed with her new husband that she excludes everyone else—even her own daughter—from her life. She longs for her old relationship with her mom.

▲ Michael is a middle-aged gay man whose twenty-year relationship with Jack ended recently. Bereft and lonely, Michael feels especially distraught because he can't risk expressing his sense of loss in a culture that usually refuses to acknowledge, much less accept, the reality of gay relationships.

▲ George worked for decades at the same company. His track record as a loyal, high-performing executive, however, didn't spare him from the consequences of corporate downsizing. Jobless for the first time ever, George feels severely traumatized; he has lost not only his financial stability but also his means of self-definition and his network of professional relationships.

▲ Jan experienced the loss of several lovers. Every time Jan established what she hoped would be a close relationship, her sister, Lydia, showed up and "stole" the new man. Now Jan feels betrayed both by her lovers and by Lydia.

▲ Alicia reveled in her role as a grandmother and spent long hours caring for her son's three children. When her son got divorced, however, his ex-wife gained custody of the children. Alicia's former daughter-in-law denied Alicia access to her grandchildren. The loss of contact has hit Alicia as hard as if someone had denied her contact with her own kids.

Why do so many men and women find themselves struggling with the aftermath of failed relationships? Why, in short, are there so many brokenhearted people? And what can you do if you find yourself in a similar position, wondering how to pick up the pieces when an important part of your life—perhaps *the* most important part—has collapsed?

In the chapters that follow, I'll offer several answers to this question, as well as detailed suggestions for how to mend a broken heart. As a starting point, however, I'll examine one common cause and its consequences.

". . . And They Lived Happily Ever After"

Among the words that do the most damage to human relationships are those concluding many fairy tales. By implying that love solves all problems and that the bond between two people will last forever, the classic final line ". . . and they lived happily ever after" creates expectations that few relationships can possibly meet. Countless people have experienced frustration, sadness, and pain when the realities of their human ties fall short of fantasy. The result is a legacy of shattered dreams and broken promises. And although this legacy isn't by any means the sole cause of people's heartache, it's such a significant contributor that we should explore its effects before we consider any other issues.

We've all been barraged by the happily-ever-after message from the earliest years of childhood onward. Fairy tales are only the first of many ways by which we get the message. Other kinds of children's books are common sources, too. Books and magazines for adults provide another powerful medium for spreading the word. (Think of all the articles in women's magazines that are variations on the theme of finding Mr. Right.) Movies are extremely powerful as well, ranging from Disney animations to romantic comedies to three-hankie tearjerkers. In addition, parental expectations and behavior play a large role in forming our images of relationships. This behavior can take an overt form, such as parents' asking their daughters, "Why don't you find a nice young man who'll marry you and make you happy?" It can be more subtle, too, such as parents' responding to their sons' or daughters' choice of partner in ways that convey approval or disapproval more indirectly. If parents have bought into the fairy-tale messages and lived their lives accordingly, their behavior provides a powerful example for their children. Combined, these various forms of happily-ever-after attitudes create a deep and persistent message that no one in our culture fully escapes.

Here's a real-life example. Jeff, a bachelor businessman, had achieved success in the corporate world, yet he felt desperately unhappy. Wealth, professional acclaim, and a jet-set social life failed to satisfy him.

Then, at the age of thirty-five, Jeff noticed a framed photograph while shopping in a posh camera shop. The person in the photo was the most beautiful woman he had ever seen. Jeff felt an immediate sense of longing for her and, in addition, an overwhelming intuition that she was the woman of his dreams. Ever since boyhood, Jeff had always wanted to find his one-and-only perfect love. Now he felt confident that this mystery woman would fulfill his deepest longings.

It turned out that the camera shop's proprietor had photographed the woman himself. Requesting information, Jeff met with initial resistance. He eventually prevailed, however, persuading the merchant to provide the woman's phone number. Her name was Hallie. Jeff met her within a few weeks and, to his surprise and delight, discovered that she responded warmly to his romantic interest. They ended up marrying within a few months.

Jeff and Hallie didn't live happily ever after. On the contrary, the prince and his princess bride struggled with each other from the first years of wedded life. They raised a large family, but many conflicts cropped up between them—conflicts for which prior experiences, including their unhappy childhoods, left them ill prepared to understand or resolve. The realities of marriage bore no resemblance to what both Jeff and Hallie had expected. Each felt disappointed, angry, and resentful toward the other.

As their children grew up, the legacy of the parents' expectations fell to the next generation. What Jeff and Hallie's kids witnessed was a relationship that they believed would work out precisely because it was a fairy tale come true. The prince had rescued the princess: Hallie, who was beautiful but poor, married Jeff, who was Mr. Success. She gained security; he gained his trophy wife. Unfortunately, the fairy-tale ending just didn't come about.

Jeff and Hallie are now divorced. Three of their four children (currently in their early and middle twenties) have already experienced divorces, too. Despite the heartache that they saw their parents suffer, the children keep repeating the fairy-tale messages that they perceived—messages from their parents about the nature of love and human relations—and they have brought this legacy into their own lives. Not only do they have problems with intimacy, but they also have difficulty distinguishing fantasy from reality, in part because of the mixed messages they received from their parents, who tried to live out a fairy tale rather than an ordinary, imperfect human relationship.

As a psychotherapist, I consider fairy tales to be a double-edged sword. They can instruct and entertain; at the same time, they can prompt us to believe damaging and unrealistic messages that end up dormant in our unconscious minds yet often played out in our conscious, everyday lives, particularly in our romantic relationships. A girl imagines being rescued by a prince and riding off into the sunset. . . . A boy imagines finding a beautiful princess who will adore him and meet his every need. . . . On the surface, it's all very charming and romantic. Unfortunately, fairy tales never talk about the reality of living with another person, building a life together, raising children, dealing with economic stress and hardship, developing a mutually fulfilling sex life, or coping with power struggles in a relationship.

"... And they lived happily ever after." But fairy tales don't tell you how that's done.

Five Destructive Beliefs About Love and Loss

Five common but damaging beliefs foster this legacy of loss. These beliefs are the stuff that fairy tales are made of—images of love and relationships that we are all socialized to believe and take to heart. Although few people actually experience a state of living happily ever after, these images are, in fact, manifested in how we think, feel, and behave in our relationships.

BELIEF #1:
You have one and only one perfect love.

We speak of soul mates, of marriages that are "made in heaven." It's tempting to believe that each person has a single true partner who will meet all needs and soothe all hurts. Is this true, though? And if not, why is this belief so tenacious?

Part of the answer is that as children we generally have only one set of parent-child bonds, one with a mother, one with a father. The parent-child bond exerts a continuing and understandably powerful effect on our perception of human relationships throughout life. Our culture—especially popular culture—reinforces the belief in one true love. (Think of the myriad songs, books, and movies that hinge on someone finding his or her still-undiscovered one true love.) The truth is, the parent-child bond isn't the proper paradigm for other human relationships. You have one mom or one dad, but there's more than just one potential soul mate or lover in your life.

In actuality, there are many people you could love, and there are many people who could love you—many potential partners who could help you attain happiness if you gave them a chance.

In addition to being a strong cultural belief, the notion of one true love is also a psychological defense mechanism. If you believe that you have only one perfect love, you can resist getting involved with others. This is a particularly likely attitude if you've been badly hurt. If you believe that you have one true love, and if you've been hurt by divorce, loss, or separation, then your belief becomes a way of keeping yourself from recommitting and loving some other person. Your belief becomes a way to protect yourself from getting hurt. Unfortunately, it's also a way to live the rest of your life in isolation.

Julia, who is thirty-five years old, doesn't stay in relationships more than a couple of months. Although she starts love affairs with great enthusiasm, she soon finds flaws in each new partner, which gives her the perfect excuse to bail out. One man is too emotionally reserved; another is too effusive. One bores her, another acts possessive, and another has an irritating laugh. Julia can't seem to find someone who meets her admittedly high expectations.

The men in Julia's life may or may not be fatally flawed as potential partners. Regardless of their deficiencies, however, part of Julia's problem is her fear of intimacy and abandonment. Losses that Julia experienced during childhood now manifest themselves in her present-day relationships. As a result, Julia keeps falling passionately in love, convincing herself that *this* man is the perfect person, and then realizing as reality sets in that this person is in fact imperfect—at which point she dumps him. Her wish for perfect oneness repeatedly obstructs her from having a meaningful relationship.

Why does this happen? Is Julia's problem simply that she believes all the fairy tales she keeps hearing over the years? Fairy-tale messages are certainly part of the problem. At the same time, there's also a deeper, more primordial reason that Julia longs for a perfect, unflawed relationship. In a sense, Julia is longing for the symbiosis of the mother-infant bond. Infants have a biological need for being totally fulfilled, totally nurtured. Without that need and the means to express it (such as crying urgently when hungry) an infant would be unable to make his or her needs known. The mother-infant bond fulfills that need. However, the situation is dramatically different for adults. To be healthy adults, lovers cannot be two sides of a symbiotic relationship. People are human; no one is perfect. We are all imperfect. But if you have suffered great losses during childhood— the death of a parent, for instance, or perhaps a sense of loss resulting from a parent's absence or incompetence—you may end up longing for a level of perfection that you never received from Mother or Father.

For some people, another element comes into play. Longing for the one true love may be a way of coping with fear of your own imperfections. Rather than accepting human limitations both in yourself and the other person, you may demand perfection as a way of avoiding your own humanity. You may feel terribly imperfect, so you look for the perfect person to build up your ego and help you to feel whole. One way or the other, these kinds of beliefs and fantasies don't make for good, realistic, healthy relationships.

BELIEF #2:
If you love someone with all your heart and soul, and if you give that person all your love and loyalty, everything will work out and no one will get hurt.

The most straightforward expression of this belief is the saying Love conquers all. This and other sayings promise that no matter how vast the distances separating you and your lover, no matter how great the obstacles between you, and no matter how serious the problems confronting you, you can prevail simply by loving each other. Unfortunately, this belief has little grounding in reality. Love doesn't conquer all, and love alone won't solve your problems. Here are two examples of how this love-conquers-all belief wreaks havoc on people's lives.

Bob and Kim

Bob and Kim met in college, fell in love, and married right after graduation. Each of them saw the other as an anchor in a stormy, dangerous world, for both had suffered early, significant losses. Bob's mother had died when he was seven. Kim's dad was alcoholic, abusive, critical, detached, and cold. As a result, Kim and Bob found great solace in each other's company.

Yet their past experiences set them up for a problematic relationship. Because Kim's role in her own family had been that of the nurturer and peacemaker—the daughter who would try to calm her angry father and console her beleaguered mother—Kim strove to become the perfect caregiver for Bob, who felt damaged by his early loss of a parent. Bob in turn saw Kim as the perfect one true love he'd longed for ever since his mother died. Were they aware of the dynamic they had set up? Almost certainly not. But their lack of awareness didn't make the dynamic any less powerful; on the contrary, doing what they did *without* awareness of their motivations made their actions all the more powerful. Bob and Kim were just doing what they'd learned to do all along. Bob was casting about for a female figure to provide the love and nurturance he'd never received. Kim was trying to find a partner who was vulnerable, weak, and emotionally distant, just like her dad—a perfect therapy project for her to undertake and use to avoid getting her own needs met.

It's not hard to see why Bob latched on to Kim. He had experienced one of the most devastating losses that a human being can suffer, a young child's loss of a parent. His emotional needs were so intense and so deep that he had established a long-standing pattern of acquiring surrogate mothers to nurture him. In some respects, Kim was simply the latest of a long series of women who had taken Bob under their wings.

What of Kim, though? After enduring her dad's unreliability, dismissiveness, rage, and abusiveness, why would she tolerate more of the same from someone else? Another needy, damaged male was the last thing she needed. The truth, however, is that Kim's choice of Bob as her spouse makes perfect (though not healthy) sense. Without her knowing it, Kim married Bob partly to complete her unfinished business. Kim believed that she could get this detached, elusive man—a man who is very much like her father—to love her just as she'd wanted Dad to love her. The first time around she had failed; now Bob was a second chance. She thought that if she loved him with all her heart and soul, and if she were loyal enough and good enough, then this time everything would work out. She wouldn't feel hurt. Love would conquer all. Kim would emerge victorious.

Unfortunately, things didn't work out that way. Bob and Kim ended up having two children, and they stayed married almost ten years. However, because of Bob's erratic participation in the marriage (not to mention his abuse of alcohol), the couple encountered severe problems. Kim responded to Bob's remoteness and hostility by trying to please him in every way. Bob found Kim's subservience contemptible and claustrophobic, which prompted him to withdraw still further. Tensions increased as the marital interactions spun out of control. Bob eventually ended up having several extramarital affairs; after a major confrontation with Kim, he abandoned his family. The marriage ultimately broke up. Bob remains an active alcoholic and doesn't support his ex-wife or kids.

Ruth and Gerald

Gerald, a successful businessman, fell in love with a younger woman named Ruth. In itself, his marriage fulfilled one of Gerald's fondest dreams: to have a youthful, lovely wife. Ruth happened to come from a troubled background—her mother and father were icy, unloving parents—but her past prompted Gerald to love Ruth all the more intensely. Ruth's sad family history fed Gerald's dream, for he not only found his princess but rescued her as well.

The fantasy lasted forty years. Gerald and Ruth married and raised a family. To all outward appearances, they were successful members of society. They lived in a fancy house, owned lots of possessions, and mingled with the high and mighty. Inwardly, however, Ruth and Gerald had another story. Ruth's emotionally deprived background made it difficult for her to maintain intimacy with her husband. She avoided him and sought refuge in parties, clubs, and high society. She was subject to severe depressions but unwilling to seek counseling or psychotherapy. She was dependent on Gerald in many ways yet resentful of him for being what she perceived as the crutch she depended on.

Gerald, meanwhile, was out in the real world, trying to find some sort of solid ground for his marriage. He believed that if only he could be good enough—if he sent Ruth flowers more often, if he earned more money and took her on more trips, if he bought her more clothes, a bigger house, or more jewelry—if he did all this (and more), everything would work out. That's how he would prove his love for his empty, lonely wife. He would be the mother and father that Ruth had never had.

But once again it didn't work. Gerald couldn't be his wife's mother and father. He couldn't even be her psychotherapist (although a properly trained therapist might have been part of what Ruth needed). And no matter how hard Gerald might try, love couldn't conquer all.

The Limits of Love
The reason that love doesn't conquer all is that love alone doesn't take into account the complexities of each relationship or of each person's personality development. It doesn't take into account family histories. It doesn't take into account individual coping mechanisms for stress and resiliency. And it doesn't take into account the mundane details of an everyday relationship. Romantic notions and expectations simply don't provide a couple with enough tools for dealing with the pressures that they face.

When the primary driving force within a relationship is fantasy, your real understanding of your partner tends to be overshadowed by a set of preconceived images rather than by open-minded perceptions of the other person. The result is that you may find fault with your partner for falling short of an illusion instead of seeing the illusion as a mere approximation or ideal. You and your partner may feel resentful of each other and disappointed by each other's limitations, and you may be disappointed by your own inability to coax, prod, cajole, or force your partner into conforming to the ideal.

BELIEF #3:
If love feels familiar to what you experienced in childhood, it must be the real thing.

This, too, is a common belief. Far from being a sign of a healthy emotional bond, however, it may in fact signal what psychoanalytically trained therapists call a *repetition compulsion*, a tendency to repeat patterns of behavior established earlier in life, even when the behavior is inappropriate (and possibly counterproductive) in the present. In many cases, what people are trying to do is attain an unattainable love object. If you had a difficult relationship with one or both of your parents, for example, you may end up repeatedly establishing relationships with people who share your parents' qualities. Your ties with such people may suggest an inadvertent effort to win your parents' affection and approval, though it may be decades since your earlier parent-child relationship ended.

Jamie
Jamie is a fairly typical example of someone affected by this belief. Jamie is the only daughter in a family with many sons. Although her mother always doted on her, Jamie's father openly favored her brothers. During her childhood, Jamie found her father demanding and aloof. She felt a constant need to prove her worthiness, yet she never felt that she received enough approval or affection. In fact, nothing

she did ever pleased her father. Her father wasn't abusive—simply so remote that Jamie often wondered if he even noticed her, much less loved her.

Once she reached adulthood, Jamie felt that she had outgrown this situation. She attained her long-sought career goal—to become a successful trial lawyer—and she engaged in a series of love affairs with wealthy, accomplished, influential men. In spite of her external success, however, Jamie does not feel happy with her life. Her legal career seems like one struggle after another, a constant effort to prove herself before judges (usually male) as she combats her adversaries (mostly male). Her love life disappoints her, too, since her lovers, though powerful and rich, often turn out to be far less emotionally responsive than she hopes. Jamie often wonders why she feels so unhappy despite having disengaged from her overbearing, icy father.

The truth is that she hasn't disengaged from Dad at all. Jamie is still caught in his thrall. Far from having eliminated Dad's influence from her life, she remains captive to his expectations and to her own desire to please him. This is true both for her career and her love life. Although Jamie chose a profession far different from her father's, it involves an almost constant reenactment of a childhood pattern: presenting arguments and evidence to a presiding older male as a means for winning his approval at the expense of competing younger males. Even her search for affection lives out the same drama of Jamie striving almost endlessly for the love of an older man who eventually slights or ignores her.

Jamie's experience shows how the repetition compulsion can work in real life. The theory of the repetition compulsion (suggested in Sigmund Freud's work) is a way of explaining why people engage in otherwise inexplicable, often persistent behaviors. Applied to human relationships, this theory states that if a person picks a love partner who resembles someone whose love he or she is trying to regain, the person is unconsciously motivated to find a partner who fits the characteristics of the person he or she is longing for. In Jamie's case, this theory may explain her choices of her profession and of her lovers, both being aspects of life that required proving her own worthiness to aloof males.

There are two types of parenting that sometimes trigger this phenomenon. One involves a caregiver (usually a parent, often the mother) who is *sometimes available*; the other involves a caregiver who is *never available*.

The sometimes-available caregiver is erratic, inconsistent, unreliable—sometimes attentive but sometimes not. This is the classic setup for people who, during adulthood, choose come-here-go-away types of partners. (By *come-here-go-away types* I mean people who alternately or even simultaneously demand attention or affection yet reject what is offered.) Although the experience of receiving care from an erratic, inconsistent parent is often painful, it becomes familiar. People accustomed to this experience then often seek something similar later in life, which may lead to relationships that to some degree repeat the past. Jamie manifests this tendency by her choice of lovers, who tend to be emotionally unpredictable. Some of them were distant from start to finish. Others were charming and outwardly engaged with her but wary of real intimacy. A few wavered from passionate possessiveness to abusive rage.

The never-available caretaker produces a different effect. Men and women raised by such parents tend to grow up rather disconnected or remote from their own feelings. Having spent their childhood years in a state of emotional starvation, they have adjusted to this early scarcity of love by learning to do without. They often have a difficult time being intimate with other people. This lack of intimacy is a way of repeating the experience of their first difficult intimate relationship. They're detached and hard to reach. Some show a predisposition toward addictions, whether to work, drugs, alcohol, or sex.

Lawrence

An example of a person affected by a never-available caretaker is Lawrence, now forty-two, whose depressive mother raised him without support from her husband, a ne'er-do-well who spent little time with the family. Lawrence's mother had such severe psychological problems that she possessed no emotional energy for parenting tasks. Simply keeping a job often exceeded her grasp; providing emotional sustenance for a child wasn't even a possibility. Lawrence learned to survive in this stark environment. During adolescence, however, he did poorly and often acted out in school. He pulled his life together somewhat during adulthood but never thrived either in a career or in a relationship. He maintains sporadic relationships with women but has yet to marry or start a family. To this day, Lawrence lives an outwardly normal life—he has a job, a house, and a scattering of friends—but there's only minimal depth to his interpersonal commitments.

The parental care you received as a child created a pattern that feels familiar to you. If you received consistent, supportive care, that is the pattern you will associate with intimate relationships. If you received erratic, unpredictable care, that will become part of your pattern. If you received no care at all, you will probably expect the same absence of love and attention from other relationships. In short, your early experiences of love become a psychological map for how love feels. If love in your adult relationships feels like your early love experiences, then it must be the real thing. It must be love. And you will probably feel a drive to repeat this pattern. Much of this process is unconscious; nevertheless, you're driven and pulled to capture once again what you experienced long ago.

There's another dimension present, too: you hope that now you're going to do it even better. You're going to obtain the unobtainable love object. You're going to make the person you love stay with you, love you forever, and never hurt you. This time, you're not going to fail.

You can see the implication—there's unfinished business. As an infant, you felt a hunger to be fed both emotionally and physically. If this drive to be fed hasn't been satisfied, there's an empty space (what some people colloquially call a "hole in the soul") that can remain for years, decades, even a whole lifetime. If this emotional state is sufficiently powerful, it can motivate us to seek people who often are incapable and unavailable—people who can't give us what we need, just as our childhood caregivers couldn't.

The Influence of Siblings

There's another important issue to consider. Although your parents probably had the greatest influence on your early development, other people are powerful influences as well. If you had brothers or sisters, they almost certainly played a part in how you now perceive relationships and human interactions, including love. Sibling interactions are extremely significant determinants of human personality. Some psychological research suggests, for instance, that relationships with siblings have a major influence on a person's choice of a marital partner. In general, too, sibling relationships can profoundly affect how you perceive other people. If a woman has a warm, nurturing bond with her brothers, for instance, she may well be predisposed toward comfortable relationships with other men. If, on the other hand, she has experienced hostility or abuse from her brothers, her unpleasant sibling bonds may negatively influence her perceptions of male-female relationships. Under other circumstances, such as when a child experiences the loss of a sibling through death or custody disputes, the experience may be devastating.

BELIEF #4:
If you keep busy, you will be able to avoid, deny, or diminish your problems.

It's tempting to imagine that your sense of loss will go away if you ignore it. Sometimes this behavior suggests the psychological defense mechanisms called *denial* and *displacement*. Faced with a frustrating, threatening, or troubling situation, you may respond by ignoring the situation, by denigrating its significance, or by focusing on other events to distract yourself. An example would be a woman who excuses her husband's abusive behavior by explaining (to herself or others) that he's under a lot of pressure at work. If she just "tries to be good," her husband will feel less hassled and will hold his temper. In short, people often tend to rationalize and protect themselves against the problems facing them.

Denial

Denial is deeply ingrained in our culture. You're expected to suppress or avoid your feelings. Because feelings can stir you up, they complicate other people's expectations of how they want you to behave and feel. The most common message you may hear following a loss is Get over it. As a result, you're socialized to deny your feelings or to avoid them by keeping busy, being strong, and keeping a stiff upper lip. You're encouraged to keep moving, keep going, and not give in to those feelings. If you succumb, you'll be weakened and vulnerable. Grow up, pull yourself together, get moving. As a result of these social messages, you may find it difficult to stay in touch with your feelings.

Denial is basically a way of pretending that an event isn't really happening, isn't as bad as it seems, or isn't really happening to *you*. It's a way of protecting yourself from the problems you're experiencing—death, divorce, illness, problems at work, problems in your marriage, problems with your kids, or problems with friends. If you don't think about what's happening, maybe it'll go away. Maybe it'll change. Or maybe you can change the situation. Facing your feelings realistically is very difficult; it's painful to look at the reality of the situation and come to terms with it.

For example, consider a little girl who is growing up in an alcoholic family. The girl's mother is out all night long, drinking and partying with men, but she tells her daughter she's working late at the office. Which version do you think the girl is more likely to believe? She's much more likely to believe that her mother is working late, not that her mother has a drinking problem or is promiscuous. The girl's denial maintains her fantasy bond to her mother. It's less painful and less scary for a child. Because she's so dependent on her mother, the girl doesn't have many choices.

Denial can become a pattern of behavior that continues well past childhood, however. When your unconscious is already patterned to deny or diminish problems or to pretend the problems aren't happening, you're most likely to repeat those problems from early childhood.

Displacement

Joe is an example of someone who used displacement to avoid his problems. Joe had worked hard for many years to advance his career; eventually he succeeded in meeting his goals. Then, suddenly, his wife told him that she was leaving him for another man. Instead of pulling back, working less, going to therapy, or at least trying to feel a sense of loss about his failed marriage, Joe put his energies into avoiding what had happened and what he felt about it. He worked even more furiously to avoid his painful feelings. Unfortunately, his feelings emerged in other ways. He felt depressed, anxious, unable to concentrate, and prone to headaches, colds, and back pain. Although he tried avoiding his emotions, he couldn't escape them. Eventually Joe suffered a mental breakdown. He started seeing a psychiatrist, who put him on antianxiety and antidepressant drugs. Although initially regarding these developments as signs of personal failure, Joe soon started to see them as a necessary step to pulling his life together. He began to grieve the loss of his marriage. In addition—and perhaps more important—Joe started to grieve some of the childhood losses that led him to the workaholic behavior that proved so damaging to his marriage in the first place.

Denial and displacement are common. They are culturally based responses to problems and consistent with many American values. We're told Work hard. Don't give in to your feelings. Shrug off your troubles and get on with life. Unfortunately, this damn-the-torpedoes attitude is often counterproductive. Denying what you feel can take a severe toll on your life and on others' lives, too. Displacing your grief, anger, or frustration onto something or someone else can do tremendous damage.

Consider Joe again. He displaced a lot of his anger onto relationships following his divorce. He became critical of the women he knew and obsessed with controlling his relationships with them. Displacement took over much of his responses to people because he was in denial; he never felt overtly angry about what had happened with his wife or about what had gone on in his childhood. He pretended that it didn't matter. He claimed that he wasn't really angry at all. But by rationalizing his wife's behavior he became a nonperson, invisible even to himself. In the process, he abandoned himself; he was totally out of touch with his feelings. And anyone who is totally out of touch with his or her feelings will probably displace those feelings and direct them at other people or else act them out in destructive ways.

BELIEF #5:
If bad things happen, then you must have caused them.

Jeremy and Lynn, who are lovers, had a severe quarrel one evening. As the couple's communication deteriorated, Jeremy stomped out of Lynn's apartment in a rage, got into his car, and roared away. Lynn didn't hear from him until several hours later, when Jeremy called her from the local emergency room following a car accident. He wasn't severely injured, but he had broken a few ribs and suffered a bad case of whiplash. In the aftermath of this accident, Lynn blamed herself for her lover's misfortune: if only she hadn't accused Jeremy of so many things, he wouldn't have raced off and totaled his car. She felt tremendous guilt over what had taken place.

Events like Jeremy and Lynn's experience aren't at all uncommon. Not only do people suffer many kinds of misfortune, but their relatives, spouses, lovers, and friends frequently take on the burden of what has happened. If you've experienced something similar to this, you may have felt not only *concern* but also *responsibility*. You may feel that you caused the accident, illness, or other calamity rather than believing that the misfortune was a coincidence or the result of your partner's own actions.

What I'm describing here suggests an attitude similar to *magical thinking*. Common in childhood but sometimes appearing in adulthood, magical thinking prompts a belief that merely thinking good or ill of someone can bring about desired or dreaded events. (For instance, a boy who screams "I hate you!" at his mother during an argument may fear that he caused his mother's subsequent illness.)

Children engage in magical thinking for two reasons.

One is that in actuality children often feel helpless, unable to cope with the situations and people around them, including their parents. Magical thinking is a way of compensating for this sense of helplessness, thus allowing them to feel more powerful than they really are. This process is unconscious.

The second reason is that parents often *do* blame their children for causing specific problems. They may not do so directly, but they do so all the same. Somehow parents give their children the message that they are burdensome; their needs are too great. Especially when coping with problems and feeling stressed, parents can behave in narcissistic ways. At such times, the parents may not be emotionally (or even physically) available to their kids. They aren't as attentive as they could be or want to be. When that kind of isolation affects a child, he or she tends to internalize the parent's criticism and regard it as his or her own fault.

To complicate matters, the child may feel that if he or she caused the problems, then he or she has the power to control or cure them. Lynn was appalled by Jeremy's injuries resulting from the accident. As if she hadn't taken on enough guilt already (a well-established pattern in their relationship), she then proceeded to assign herself responsibility for her lover's total rehabilitation. Neither the original accident nor its eventual resolution were Lynn's exclusive burden to carry. Just as she isn't necessarily to blame because things went wrong, she doesn't have sole responsibility for making them right again.

▲ △ ▲

All five of these beliefs hold sway over us. Regrettably, they can do great damage. The result is that most of us—no matter how intelligent, insightful, professionally accomplished, and outwardly realistic—live at least partly in a state of fantasy about other people. And the result is a heightened state of vulnerability when a relationship ends.

Why are these fairy-tale beliefs so destructive to you? One reason is that the fairy-tale view of human nature allows you a diminished opportunity to create nurturing, stable, healthy relationships. The fairy-tale view is idealistic, but mostly in negative ways. It's hard to tolerate an ordinary man's or woman's eccentricities and imperfections if you have your heart set on the perfect prince or princess. It's difficult to stay patient with the normal ups and downs of relationships when you're intent on living happily ever after. Fairy-tale images of love can, in fact, become an addiction in their own right. If you're so attached to these kinds of fantasies, you're not living altogether in the real world. You may feel continuously enticed by the highs of an intoxicating, exhilarating relationship; when reality sets in, you may feel acutely disappointed.

This dynamic is especially destructive when a relationship ends. If you're expecting to live happily ever after, you may fall pretty hard when your spouse, lover, friend, or relative is gone. You're much more at risk when you've subscribed to these fairy-tale beliefs—more at risk of picking the wrong person, staying in a damaging relationship too long, and losing touch with what you need from yourself and from the world around you.

In the aftermath of a relationship collapsing, you're in a heightened state of vulnerability. This is almost inevitable, and it's not necessarily a bad thing—painful, but not necessarily bad. Why? Because the end of the relationship is an opportunity to decide what's possible for you by reflecting on the past and understanding your patterns of behavior and their origin so that you don't repeat them. However, you should keep in mind that this vulnerability may lead you to

- ▲ hook up too quickly with another (and possibly inappropriate) partner
- ▲ engage in compulsive behaviors, including overeating, abuse of drugs or alcohol, or compulsive sex
- ▲ feel lonely, insecure, empty, or depressed
- ▲ "put up walls" and avoid intimacy, blocking out the possibility of connecting with other people

Keep in mind that these are all common reactions. You're feeling wounded. It's understandably tempting to hook up with another wounded person, seek the solace of drugs or alcohol, or isolate yourself altogether. However, such responses to loss can complicate your recovery, perhaps severely; in some cases, they can lead to far more serious problems than those you face already.

What should you do, then? Before I answer that question, I'll explore in more detail other people's experiences of loss. Then I'll proceed to examine the nature of loss and how to deal with it.

PART II

Real People, Real Problems

When I travel around the country giving workshops and lectures, I hear from many brokenhearted people who are suffering from a great variety of losses. Many failed to see the problems in their relationships and then woke up one day and found that these relationships had ended. Some of these people are husbands, wives, or lovers whose partners have moved out—either physically, emotionally, or both—and are devastated as a result. Others are men and women whose losses are less socially recognized. Some are gay men or lesbians whose pain following rejection is essentially the same as what heterosexuals experience, except that their grief, anger, and frustration are often less accepted by society in general, hence more likely to be suppressed or hidden. Some are parents who will have less time with their children as a consequence of postdivorce custody settlements. Some are grandparents who won't be able to see their grandchildren often enough (if at all) in the aftermath of an adult son's or daughter's divorce. Still others are friends grieving the loss of a friendship because the friends are growing apart or because of the complex aftermath of loss through divorce or death. Still others are sisters and brothers traumatized by a sibling rift. All are real people who have experienced real suffering.

Part II of *How to Mend a Broken Heart* chronicles a variety of losses. None of the following stories is greatly detailed; each is simply a sketch of how one or more people have experienced a relationship and its eventual end. My purpose in presenting these stories is to suggest both the variety of what people feel following the loss of an important relationship and, simultaneously, to portray the elements common to all experiences of loss. My intention is to provide you with a feeling that your emotions are normal—something shared with many other people. In addition, these stories serve as reference points for discussions throughout later chapters of *How to Mend a Broken Heart*.

Feel free to pick and choose among the stories, selecting some to read while ignoring others. As I'll discuss in Part III, almost all losses share significant features regardless of the specific human details, and people's individual experiences of grief usually share certain features, too. For this reason, it's possible to learn from almost anyone's loss. For the moment, however, follow your hunches about which of these stories apply or don't apply to your own situation.

1

$\mathscr{A}$nnette and Jack—
A Marriage Unravels

$\mathbf{A}$mong Americans, approximately 50 percent of all marriages now end in divorce, and countless nonmarital relationships dissolve as well. Many couples willingly choose to part company, of course, and a shared decision of this sort may result in far less hurt, anger, and acrimony than would a decision in which one partner rejects the other. Even the most amicable end to a love relationship, however, often creates profound emotions, including sadness, depression, and a sense of deprivation. In my years as a therapist, I've seen very few marriages or love affairs end without one or both partners feeling some kind of loss.

Annette Sanderson and Jack Bauer met during their first year at college. They fell in love "at first sight," as both admit, and were almost inseparable from the start of their relationship. Friends called them the Golden Couple because they seemed to have hit the jackpot in every possible way. Both were attractive, talented, capable, ambitious people. They clearly loved each other and shared with their friends the high spirits that their love created. When they married right after graduation, Jack and Annette seemed ready to live a fairy-tale life that others coveted for their own relationships but could never quite attain.

The Bauers did, in fact, do well together for many years. They thrived in their careers—Annette as the marketing manager for a software company, Jack as chief information officer at a large insurance firm. They started a family—two girls and a boy. They enjoyed a comfortable suburban life in the Midwest. Prospering in many ways, the Bauers had every reason to believe that their fairy tale had come true.

Yet eventually, shadows crept into this sunny landscape. Most of what befell Annette and Jack was simply the consequence of cumulative stress, middle-age anxiety, and errors of judgment. If the Bauers had anticipated a bumpy ride, they might well have ridden through their difficulties without much damage; perceiving themselves as the Golden Couple, however, left them expecting few or no problems throughout life. They were both poorly prepared to deal with the fairly routine difficulties facing them.

Financial pressures and the demands of family life prompted the Bauers to allot most parental duties to Annette and most of the breadwinner's role to Jack. In theory, this wasn't a problem—simply their choice as a married couple—but in practice, each spouse lost touch with what the other's tasks demanded on a day-to-day basis. Annette felt progressively more and more isolated at home. Jack felt more and more trapped in his professional role. Each spouse gradually believed that he or she carried a larger burden than the other, and neither could understand the challenges and problems that the other faced.

Meanwhile, another element influenced their behavior as husband and wife: the gravitational force that their family histories exerted on them individually and as a couple. For Jack, the big issue was anger at his mother. Jack's mother, though thoughtful and loving in many ways, had tended to be overly controlling of Jack during his childhood. As a result, Jack had generally responded to his mother with a mixture of longing and rage—with longing because he craved her unconditional maternal love more than anything else, with rage because he resented his own powerlessness and dependency on the woman he longed for.

Jack had a vague awareness of his past without a clear sense of how it affected him during adulthood. He tended to believe, in fact, that it didn't affect him at all. His childhood conflicts with his mother were now long past, he insisted; his parents lived far away and didn't affect his adult behavior. His ambivalence toward his mother, however, exerted a powerful effect on how Jack dealt with Annette. For just as he once resented a woman for controlling his behavior yet simultaneously prompting feelings of dependency, Jack now resented Annette's demands and influence, too.

Annette's childhood was happier than Jack's but not without its own troubling side effects. Her family was relatively well-off and happy. At the same time, Annette's mother's parental role (which involved raising seven children almost singlehandedly) left her physically exhausted yet unwilling to set limits on her children and her husband. This legacy of all-tolerant motherhood left Annette with a nearly impossible image of what she herself should attain. On a deep level, Annette believed that she had no choice but to give and give and give. Both Annette and Jack tended to be constrained, at times almost imprisoned, by family expectations.

Sometimes Jack and Annette tried working through the difficulties facing them, but they never seemed to get very far. They hadn't needed to exert themselves in the past; it seemed awkward to start now. Weren't things just supposed to sort themselves out? Surely, they believed, a Golden Couple shouldn't have to make an effort in the first place.

Unfortunately, both Jack and Annette felt a deep, restless anger that they could neither identify nor ignore. Life was difficult. The pressures on them exceeded what they had anticipated. Each spouse wanted to honor his or her commitment to each other and their children, yet both felt nearly crushed by the demands of marriage and parenthood. Sometimes rage surged to the surface like lava from the depths.

This wasn't how things were supposed to turn out. Jack and Annette had always seen their relationship as special, a bond somehow exempt from the problems and difficulties that other couples faced. Their friends and relatives had assured them that they were blessed in some extraordinary way. Why, then, was marriage so difficult? Why did it take so much work? All these stresses and problems made no sense. If Jack and Annette were the Golden Couple, why did they end up struggling over so many issues? Their life together was a constant series of negotiations. Work, kids, money, plans, sex—everything seemed to create disagreements, discussions, more disagreements, and more discussions. Something must have been wrong, Annette figured, if she and Jack couldn't just get along effortlessly. Any relationship that required so much attention must have been seriously flawed after all.

When Jack admitted to having an affair with a woman at the insurance firm, Annette threw him out of the house. Jack, feeling humiliated and defensive, refused at first to apologize or make amends. He moved in with a bachelor friend for several days and maintained contact with his family by phone. Then, missing his children and feeling contrite toward his wife, Jack pleaded with Annette to take him back. She consented. The situation stabilized for several weeks. Soon, however, Annette discovered that Jack was continuing to see his lover. She threw him out again, this time demanding a divorce.

When their lawyers suggested marital counseling, both spouses initially refused this suggestion. Annette soon agreed to seek help, however, and contacted a counselor. Later, some of the couple's friends persuaded Jack to join Annette in the discussions, and they attended both individual and joint sessions for several months. The marriage counselor believed that the Bauers' difficulties, though intense, were not at all uncommon; if they could open up to each other, accept the need for change, and work toward common goals, they could probably solve the problems that affect many marriages during midlife.

To Jack and Annette, however, the situation seemed beyond remedy. They had always perceived themselves as the Golden Couple; how could they accept being less than that? As Annette put it,

"Things were supposed to be perfect. Now it's all ruined." And as Jack stated, "I don't see any room for compromise." The perfect image the Bauers had of marriage was unattainable. Faced with the imperfections of their own relationship, they despaired. Their counselor worked strenuously to help the couple find common ground, but neither spouse seemed willing to accommodate the other. Within a year following separation, they divorced.

The Bauers' story is lamentably common. In a culture rife with expectations of living happily ever after, men and women alike are often unprepared for the realities of marriage. Neither spouse was willing to adapt to the demands and rigors of family life. Jack's and Annette's separate personal crises—typical of many people during middle age—also complicated and ultimately destroyed their chances for reconciliation. In the years following the divorce, both Annette and Jack have experienced the complex process of recovering from loss (a process that this book will describe in detail). Annette has remarried, Jack has found a long-term romantic partner, and the ex-spouses have worked out an amicable custody arrangement for their children. They have moved on into new phases of life. To some degree, however, both Annette and Jack feel a lingering sense of sadness about the rise and fall of their marriage.

2

Sandy and Jim—
First Love and First Loss

A sense of loss can be acute even when the consequences aren't harmful over the long term, such as in the aftermath of many people's early love affairs. Most men and women engage in a series of young-adult relationships even if they ultimately settle down. Under the best of circumstances, these early relationships provide a means for exploring their own and others' emotional needs and for learning how to master the give-and-take of mature love. The tentative nature of these relationships, however, doesn't mean that they aren't intensely pleasurable while they last and intensely painful when they end.

During college, Sandy and Jim met in an art class, started dating, and fell in love. Both were young (Jim was nineteen; Sandy, just eighteen) and intensely idealistic about relationships. Both were bright, creative, and well intentioned. Both were naive—not entirely inexperienced about love and sex but still unaware of how powerfully a romantic relationship could change their lives. Neither was prepared for the intensity of what happened that year.

Their love affair took place when Jim was a second-year and Sandy a first-year student. At first they simply spent time together—studying, hanging out with friends, working on art projects, and attending campus activities. The relationship had been sexually charged from the start and turned intimate within a few weeks. This delighted both of them, for neither had experienced anything close to the physical pleasure and emotional warmth that they now shared, but the sudden transformation troubled them as well. Jim and Sandy shared a concern that they hadn't really gotten to know each other well yet. Jim worried that the intensity of the affair might jeopardize the couple's long-term stability. Everything seemed to be happening so fast. Was it possible that the sheer passion of their closeness would shake them apart? Sandy, meanwhile, felt alarmed both by this abrupt sexual involvement and by the deeper, stronger emotions she felt for this still-unfamiliar young man. Having been through several intense but dissatisfying sexual experiences in high school, she wondered if this new relationship, though in many ways more substantial than what she'd known before, would also come to grief.

The couple's backgrounds complicated the situation. Both came from families in which emotional upheaval was an element.

Jim had always been close to his parents but had endured years of harsh and sometimes abusive behavior at the hands of an emotionally disturbed older brother. As a result, he had developed a deep distrust of males his own age and, simultaneously, an intense hunger for affection and approval from girls and women. Some of these tendencies resembled what most adolescent males feel at Jim's age; the degree in Jim's case, however, was probably unusual.

Sandy's family situation had even more troubling attributes. Sandy, the only daughter in a family of five children, had always been singled out for special treatment. Even the "good" special treatment was damaging to this highly intelligent and sensitive girl, for Sandy's parents regarded her as their "little princess," granted her special privileges, and generally spoiled her. The fact that she had been astonishingly beautiful at every stage of life tended to draw attention to her from the wider world, too. Sandy had grown up convinced that the whole world was staring at her. Even the "good" attention bothered her. Some of the other kinds of treatment she had received, however, created tempestuous emotions about what the world's attention really meant: Sandy had been sexually abused since well before adolescence. Two uncles had routinely molested her from about the time she was ten years old; her father, though seemingly aware of these incidents, did nothing to stop them; and a junior high school teacher had fondled her on several occasions. Her teenage sexual experiences with several high school boyfriends did nothing to reassure Sandy about her worth as a woman.

This young couple, each with his or her own emotional wounds, now joined in a passionate relationship. It would be cynical to deny that significant good came of their time together. Both Sandy and Jim started to perceive the healing warmth that love can offer. They spent many enjoyable times in each other's company; they learned a lot about the joys and hardships of trying to communicate with another person; they shared a deep interest in art; they also started the complex adventure of exploring their own and each other's sexuality. That year was a time of tremendous growth for both of them. At the same time, it was fraught with difficulties.

Of the two, Sandy felt more conflicted about the relationship. She had spent most of her life fending off men who wanted little or nothing more than their own brief physical satisfaction; here, now, was a young man who clearly cared for her, treated her well, and felt concerned about her own happiness. This was what she said she'd always wanted but had never found. The problem was, she didn't really know how to respond. Jim's love troubled her. It seemed like a good thing, yet it felt unfamiliar, risky, worrisome. What if he, too, just wanted to use her? She didn't think she could tolerate that after getting her hopes up. Alternatively, what if he wanted more than simply exploiting her—what if he truly wanted her to be happy—at a time when Sandy couldn't respond in kind? She worried about failing him. She worried that she wasn't as good or gifted or loving as Jim thought she was. Perhaps (she thought) it would be better not to gamble on being happy at all. Perhaps it would be better to settle for the anger and unhappiness she'd known in so many other relationships.

Jim wasn't without his own emotional upheaval. Craving Sandy's love and emotional support more than anything, he became more and more possessive of her as the academic year proceeded. Surely this beautiful young woman—the China Doll, as people called her, noting her astonishingly pure features—wouldn't be satisfied with him. That concern gave him all the more reason to hang on tight, all the more reason to lavish her with affection, compliments, gifts, and attention. That way, she wouldn't even think about looking elsewhere for love.

The strain of their separate anxieties ultimately pulled Sandy and Jim apart. Sandy couldn't handle the warmth that Jim provided in such overabundance; Jim couldn't deal with Sandy's growing restlessness and curiosity about other men. By spring of that academic year, Jim and Sandy were already struggling with mutual dissatisfactions. When Jim discovered that Sandy had engaged in a series of brief sexual flings, he felt betrayed and outraged. He simply couldn't understand how she could stoop so low. They were inseparable companions! They were soul mates! Why would Sandy indulge herself in one-night stands that she admitted were pointless and unpleasant? Sandy, meanwhile, felt exasperated with Jim's possessiveness and stupid male tantrums. She would live her life as she pleased; she didn't need Jim or anyone to tell her what mattered. Within a few days, the love affair ended.

What Jim and Sandy experienced that year at college was simultaneously remarkable for them and, in the larger scheme of human experience, rather ordinary. It was not atypical of a "first love." Both Sandy and Jim were unprepared for what they went through. Burdened by problematic family histories, intense emotional needs, and inflated expectations, both felt disappointed and hurt by the outcome. Both survived the collapse of their affair. Both, in fact, grew significantly from the experience. As a result, it's easy to gloss over the young couple's feelings. The truth is, however, that both Jim and Sandy felt disoriented by their loss of one another, and many years passed before either of them understood either what had happened or how the love affair affected them for a long time afterward.

I don't regard this young couple's experience (at least in the long run) as a negative experience. On the contrary, both partners gained significantly. Both started to learn about the depth and breadth of their own and others' emotions. Both began to explore the intricacies of sex. Both glimpsed the power of family history on the present and future. Both tasted the delights of loving another person. Both discovered that even when love ended, life went on, and that they could survive to tell the tale. In short, Sandy and Jim experienced love, the loss of love, and the recovery from loss—all subjects that we'll explore throughout *How to Mend a Broken Heart*.

3

$\mathcal{W}$anda and William— Dealing with a Toxic Relationship

Another kind of loss occurs when a relationship is primarily, even overwhelmingly, negative—a burden rather than a boost to one or both partners. The collapse of this kind of relationship may be acceptable, perhaps even desirable, because continuing the relationship does more damage than good. This situation is especially clear-cut when physical or psychological abuse takes place. Unless the abusive partner can stop harming the other, the relationship is generally best ended. However, the need to end the relationship doesn't mean that the couple feels no loss in its aftermath.

Wanda and William met during high school, fell in love, and married early. By their early twenties, Wanda and William already had two daughters. Wanda spent most of her time with the couple's children; William assumed the role of breadwinner. However, William was chronically unemployed for years and kept few of his jobs longer than six months. He hadn't completed any higher education, though he attempted repeatedly to finish his undergraduate degree. His employment tended to be low-paying. As a result, he experienced a lot of frustration in trying to support Wanda and their kids while simultaneously working and studying. William worked most recently as a part-time security guard during the week and as a grocery store stock clerk over the weekends. In addition to looking after the children, Wanda also worked part-time at a nursing home.

To complicate matters, William came from a troubled family. His father, like William, lacked a trade and was in and out of work, doing odd jobs and earning a sporadic income. His mother worked at whatever employment she could find. William was one of seven siblings. His family's unmet material needs created a tense atmosphere, and William's father vented his frustrations as rage against his mother. These rage attacks and the physical form they took appalled William as a child, yet he found himself inheriting the legacy instead of rejecting it.

When William felt frustrated, he, too, tended to take out his frustration on his wife. His anger generally required little or no provocation. If Wanda looked at him the wrong way, if the pasta didn't taste just right, if the house didn't look totally neat, he hit her. Wanda generally tried to pacify William with promises and reassurances. When that approach didn't work, she suggested counseling, which William refused outright. The abuse continued off and on for years; if anything, its frequency and intensity escalated.

Wanda soon feared acutely for her safety. She often worried about the children, too, though William never physically abused them as he abused her. The family situation wasn't good even when William wasn't overtly abusive, however; the tension level was high, and Wanda felt no doubt that the children suffered from the negative emotions that permeated William and Wanda's marital relationship. The situation eventually became so disturbing that Wanda took out a restraining order on her husband. Despite her initial resolve, however, she repeatedly allowed William back into the house. She told herself to be understanding. She knew that William was disturbed, but she felt that she should try to help him. Surely she could straighten him out. Unfortunately, Wanda soon realized the risks involved in trying to be "understanding": not long ago, William beat Wanda so badly that she ended up in the hospital with contusions and a broken jawbone.

Wanda recently decided that enough is enough. She claims to love her husband, but she realizes that William is so unlikely to change that she shouldn't allow him to be part of the family. Her relationship with William now seems so hopelessly toxic that it seems best just to get away from him. She is currently trying to find a permanent living arrangement; in the meantime, she has found temporary lodging in a transitional home for abused women with children. Wanda is looking for work and is on a waiting list for housing assistance through a social service agency. She believes that the worst is over and that during the next few years she can start to rebuild her life.

She may well be right. Wanda is intent on breaking the cycle of abuse that has made her life miserable, and she feels determined to disengage from a man who, despite some good features, seems regrettably stuck in a cycle of self-contempt, frustration, and abuse. At the same time, Wanda feels tremendous confusion and sadness despite her admirable resolve. She still doesn't understand how a love relationship that started out so promisingly could have come to such a painful end. She feels uncertain about how to cut her losses and move on. She isn't even sure how to move beyond the sadness and desolation that haunt her each and every day.

I'm convinced that Wanda is acting responsibly by disengaging from William. It may well be true that on some level she still loves her husband; however, she now needs to focus on something *other* than love. It's possible to love a person but hate his or her behavior and acknowledge that the relationship is fundamentally destructive. Love won't solve Wanda's problems. Her husband is so dangerous that she must concentrate on protecting herself and her children—even if that means ignoring William's problems and, if necessary, obtaining a restraining order, seeking protection from a shelter for battered women, or taking similar steps.

As for Wanda's efforts to be "understanding," these are good-hearted but basically doomed. Wanda can't be her husband's psychotherapist. She doesn't have the training or the necessary objectivity toward William, herself, or their relationship. Playing therapist under these circumstances is a recipe for disaster. Besides, abusive partners are often highly sophisticated in manipulating others, whether by means of systematic bullying, turning on the charm, or eliciting pity. Any efforts she makes to "cure" William of his harmful behavior will almost certainly come to grief. Instead of worrying about William, Wanda should attend to the situations that she can truly change—her own life and her children's future—and relinquish her efforts to change William.

This is unquestionably a difficult situation; I won't pretend otherwise. In Part III of *How to Mend a Broken Heart*, I'll discuss similar issues, including the reasons why some people become involved with destructive partners and how you can determine which aspects of your life fall within your ability to change and which don't.

4

$\mathcal{M}$arissa and Julie—
Loss of a Lesbian Partner

Although the mainstream media continue to portray lesbian and gay relationships as either fraught with special problems or blessed with special sensitivities, most homosexual partnerships develop, proceed, and end in ways that resemble rather than differ from most heterosexual partnerships. People fall in love and out of love much the same whether they are gay or straight. People honor commitments, muddle through crises, grow, change, and sometimes betray one another. And the sense of loss that gay and lesbian partners feel when relationships end bears a striking resemblance to what heterosexuals experience under similar circumstances.

During their first ten years as lesbian partners, Marissa and Julie were happy and satisfied together. They felt deep mutual love, and they enjoyed the domestic arrangement they had created for themselves, in which Marissa, an officer at a private bank, was the couple's chief wage earner and Julie worked part-time at an art gallery but otherwise focused on keeping house. This balance of roles served them well both individually and together. After Julie and Marissa's first decade as a couple, however, both women decided that something seemed missing from their life. They wanted a child. Sizing up their options, they eventually decided to adopt a baby.

The procedures for lesbian partners in their state were complex but not entirely prohibitive; they succeeded in navigating the bureaucratic, legal, and financial course without great difficulty. Marissa's high income and legal connections smoothed the way. After no more than the usual delays and frustrations, the couple adopted a baby boy and named him Max. Both women were delighted. The only lingering frustration was that their status as unmarried partners meant that only Marissa could be the boy's legal parent.

For ten years, everything proceeded well. Marissa and Julie enjoyed parenthood tremendously; both felt comfortable with Marissa's continuing role as breadwinner and with Julie's as homemaker. Max thrived under his two mothers' care. Marissa, Julie, and Max grew together as a happy family.

Then everything fell apart. Without warning, Marissa fell in love with another woman. "I didn't want this to happen," she told Julie. "In fact, I wanted this *not* to happen. But unfortunately it *has* happened." Jane, another executive at the bank, inspired an intense love that Marissa had never experienced before. Although Marissa told Julie that her head told her to remain with her longtime lover, her heart told her to leave. And so she left.

Julie couldn't have felt more betrayed and abandoned. It wasn't just that she now lost her companion and partner of more than twenty years; she also lost her child. Marissa, being Max's adoptive mother, had the legal right to take her son when she left. The situation was fairly congenial at first: Marissa allowed Julie visitation rights. As the separation turned acrimonious, however—with escalating arguments over finances, living arrangements, and the emotional consequences of the relationship's collapse—Marissa became vindictive toward Julie. Eventually Marissa prohibited Julie from seeing Max at all. The former partners reached a stalemate that continues to this day.

The truth is that a nonadoptive partner has no legal rights as a parent. To complicate this couple's dilemma, their state does not grant a lesbian partner rights to see a son or daughter who isn't a legally adopted child. Marissa and Julie are currently in mediation to determine whether Julie will have any visitation rights at all. I'm not sure how that process will turn out. What I *do* know is that Julie feels inexpressible sadness over this situation—not just because her partner abandoned her but also because she can no longer see Max, whom she raised, nurtured, and loved for almost ten years. To make matters worse, Marissa appears to be putting Max in the middle of the situation, using him as a pawn in a game between the former partners. This kind of power play isn't uncommon, whether among gay or straight couples. It's a means by which the person who has ended the relationship sometimes justifies (at least to himself or herself) the decision to leave in the first place. One way or another, though, the result is usually just more heartbreak.

Loss is loss. What Julie has been through resembles what countless heterosexual partners experience on being rejected by a spouse or lover, just as her grief over Max's absence from her life resembles what countless parents experience on losing child visitation rights. Julie is bereaved. The only difference between what she feels and what a heterosexual person might experience is that Julie can't grieve her losses openly, since American society still tends to reject the legitimacy of homosexual partnerships. But the issues of loss and grief are fundamentally the same. The tasks that Julie faces—coming to terms with her loss and rebuilding her life—involve the same recovery process as for anyone else, a process that we'll explore thoroughly in Part III of this book.

5

$\mathcal{J}$udy and Her Parents—Loss Resulting from Alcoholism

Love partnerships are not the only ones that can leave you broken-hearted. As many people discover, other losses, too—including losses that modern American culture may not acknowledge fully, if at all—are capable of breaking your heart. Relationships with parents, siblings, and grandchildren can create a deep sense of loss and bereavement. The same holds true for relationships with in-laws and friends. Precisely because of human individuality, the end of almost *any* relationship may create a deep sense of loss.

For instance, alcoholism creates a complex legacy of disruption, uncertainty, and pain. The children of alcoholics are especially prone to a sense of loss as they struggle to cope with their parents' drinking problems, but other people—spouses, siblings, parents, friends—often feel confusion and grief, too, in dealing with an alcoholic loved one. These emotions may be unusually intense if the situation leads not only to strain on the relationship but to eventual severing of contact.

From an early age, Judy knew that her parents drank too much. She didn't know why, and she didn't know what to do about it, but she knew that their drinking changed everything in the household and always for the worse. Her mother, Alma, was especially incapacitated by her alcoholism. Her father, Will, had drunk heavily, too, but he had succeeded in his efforts to control his drinking problem; by the time Judy reached the age of thirty, Will had been sober for twenty years. Meanwhile, Alma's drinking continued to wreak havoc on the entire family.

Judy's mother never stopped denying her alcoholism. She never acknowledged that she had a problem; she continued to drink throughout the whole seventeen years of her marriage; she tried to kill herself once, taking a drug overdose while drinking heavily; she refused to enter a recovery program despite brief hospitalization following the suicide attempt. As a result, Alma's drinking was a presence in the household as demanding as a difficult and hostile family member.

Judy struggled throughout childhood, adolescence, and adulthood to figure out why her mother drank so much. Through her own efforts and through psychotherapy, she reached some insights about the situation. Her mother was emotionally immature and looked to Will to make her happy. She had very high expectations but couldn't find anything within herself that pleased her. She took no responsibility either for her children or for her marriage. Alma's own parents had been alcoholics, too, and had been chilly, even abusive, parents. Judy examined these pieces of the puzzle and found them a partial (though never altogether satisfying) explanation for her mother's dilemma. She required decades of experience and strenuously acquired insight before she could set aside the temptation—common among children of alcoholics—to blame herself. Once she reached adulthood, Judy simultaneously tried to avoid Alma and longed for her, hoping against hope that Alma would pull her life together.

Unfortunately, Alma never faced the situation or worked to overcome her alcoholism. She was often delusional, accusing her loyal husband of betrayal and ranting against Judy, her sisters, and her brother for imaginary neglect and abuse. Alma was clearly jealous of Judy and her siblings, but she refused to discuss her emotions or their probable origins. During Judy's childhood Alma would often tell her husband, "It's me or the kids." Will wouldn't abandon the kids. But once Alma started believing that Will was the cause of her problems—this occurred when Judy reached her mid-teens—Alma divorced him.

After the divorce, Alma managed to turn most of her kids against their father. Alma had gained custody of all four children despite her alcoholism. Whenever the kids visited their dad, Alma gave them the third degree, strove to make them feel guilty about seeing Will, and drove wedges between the father and his children. These divisive tactics worked temporarily but not in the long run; Judy and her three sisters resented their mother's ploys. They stayed in touch with Will despite Alma's preferences. The only son in the family rejected a relationship with his father; he was the youngest, very close to his mother, and less inclined than the others to make his own decision. The daughters all remained in contact with their dad. Alma succeeded in making her kids' lives miserable, however, including Judy's.

Throughout the many years since she left her family, Judy has struggled to make sense of her mother's behavior and its effects on Judy's life. She still longs for Alma's presence even though that presence is invariably disruptive. Judy feels that her dad's successful recovery from alcoholism has inspired her to take control of her own life. Despite her own difficulties, which include several years of marriage to an abusive husband, Judy has built a stable life for herself as a lab technician and loving parent. She enjoys her work and has a close relationship with her own daughter, Alice. A sense of pain lingers, though, when she thinks of Alma. For instance, Judy's mother has repeatedly asked to see her grandchild. Judy would like for this to be possible; unfortunately, Alma's behavior remains manipulative, unpredictable, even dangerous. As a result, Judy recently stood up to her mother and stated that she could spend time with Alice only if she stopped drinking. Alma refused. To this day, she is still prohibited from seeing her grandchild.

The situation is simultaneously painful and necessary. Judy has done what she feels is safe and healthy for her daughter. But the need to keep Alice away from her grandmother is still a source of great sadness and grief. Judy continues to struggle with the legacy of growing up in a severely troubled family. Although sympathetic in some ways toward her mother's own difficulties, Judy feels intense anger toward Alma for the hard times that her drinking caused. She has frightening dreams and flashbacks about family fights in the past. Judy sometimes worries that she, too, will eventually fall prey to alcoholism. All of these responses are typical of certain kinds of loss—responses that I will discuss in later chapters of this book.

$\mathcal{K}$aren and Her Family— Loss Resulting from a Parent-Child Rift

Family dysfunction isn't the only possible cause of a rift. Personality clashes, cultural differences, disparate expectations and goals, and ordinary misunderstandings can strain relationships. Sometimes even the love that people offer can lead to the breaking point.

Raised in a large, loving Swedish-American family, Karen Larsson felt close to her parents and siblings in many ways. She recalls her upbringing in Adamstown, Wisconsin, as delightful—an idyllic surrounding, a close-knit community, and the constant adventures of living on a family farm—and what she experienced during childhood still means a lot to her. As Karen grew up, however, she gradually grew restless in this rural community. It wasn't that she regarded her farm-town life as bad; it simply didn't provide certain experiences that became more and more important to her. Karen's interest in ballet, especially, had no outlet in Adamstown. Mr. and Mrs. Larsson disapproved of their daughter's decision to attend the University of Wisconsin at Madison, the state capital, which they regarded as a dangerous big city; they felt even more disapproval of Karen's plan to move to Chicago, where she wanted to study at a private dance academy. But ultimately what strained the parent-child relationship most severely was Karen's decision to marry a young man named Jake Eisenberg.

The Larssons are Lutherans. Having lived all their lives in a part of the country where families tended to be either Lutheran or Roman Catholic—and where religious affiliations matter so much that each group tends to socialize mostly among its own members—Mr. and Mrs. Larsson couldn't believe that their daughter could be serious about marrying a Jew. Neither of them had ever even *met* a Jew. "Of course, we're sure he's a very nice young man," Mrs. Larsson reassured Karen. Then she quickly asked, "But don't you think you should marry someone of our own kind?"

As the family controversy over Jake grew acrimonious, Karen felt more hostile rather than more responsive toward her family. Her parents' prejudices proved all of Karen's worst suspicions about them. Jake, by contrast, was everything she'd ever wanted in a mate. He was intelligent, kind, and cultured. Karen felt the pressure that her parents exerted on her, but the pressure had the opposite effect of what Mr. and Mrs. Larsson intended. Not only did Karen resolve to marry Jake, but she also decided to follow through with her plan to leave the rural Midwest. She moved to Chicago against her parents' wishes. She eloped with Jake. She settled into an urban, bohemian, independent life that was totally different from anything her family back in Adamstown could imagine.

Karen had a right to do as she chose. Unfortunately, her emotional need to prove herself complicated an already difficult situation. Her family soon felt more than simple disapproval of Karen's actions; they also felt profound hurt. To the Larssons, Karen seemed haughty about her new lifestyle, and they regarded Karen's attitude toward them as dismissive. They didn't understand her choices but saw that she felt superior to them. Then the Larssons complicated the situation further: instead of sharing their pain and sadness over what they regarded as their daughter's rejection of them and their way of life, instead of talking about their feelings and explaining that they felt belittled by her, they responded in kind. Before she could abandon them, they decided, they would abandon her. Karen's mother, especially, forcibly rejected her daughter. Mrs. Larsson decided that if Karen wanted to leave the family farm, live a bohemian life, and marry someone of a different faith, then Karen was *dead*. She was no longer part of the family. She no longer even existed.

The pain on both sides was intense. Karen felt that her family's behavior, and especially her mother's rejection, revealed even more bigotry and narrow-mindedness than she had expected. Her parents in turn felt that Karen's actions were selfish, impractical, and self-destructive. Neither side would budge. Significant family events took place among the Larssons—marriages, births, baptisms, graduations—without Karen ever receiving an invitation. The birth of Karen and Jake's children, too, came and went without either of her parents so much as sending a card of congratulations. Resentments festered, yet neither side would budge.

Looking at old family photos, Karen now feels wistful at best, often desolate. How could such an idyllic upbringing turn to dust? How could the family she loves abandon her simply for finding a wonderful man to love? How could her fairy-tale ending—a happy marriage, two lovely kids, and work she enjoys—end up suffused with sadness and loss?

I'm not sure what will come of Karen's situation. It's possible that the Larsson family will remain divided, with Karen and her parents hopelessly resentful of each other. If so, then everyone involved will perpetuate the misunderstandings, recriminations, and loss. What could be temporary narrow-mindedness may instead solidify into a tragic, permanent rift. In this case, Karen would have to cope with a complex loss. Her tasks would include accepting what seems unacceptable—her parents' rejection of her and of her creative, balanced life. Dealing with this rejection won't be easy, but Karen is so bright and capable of growth that she may well succeed.

On the other hand, it's possible that the passing years will soften all the Larssons' mutual anger and resentment. Karen seems likely to make periodic overtures to her family. Her parents may grow more openhearted as the years pass, particularly if they feel curious about their grandchildren or if one parent dies and the other (realizing that life is too short to waste on resentment) feels freer to make amends. In situations like the Larssons', siblings of an estranged family member sometimes serve as mediators between the younger and older generations. A reconciliation isn't impossible.

The outcome either way will require Karen's working through her loss as openly as possible, accepting her grief over what has happened and (as we'll see in forthcoming chapters) learning to change herself rather than attempting to change others, such as her parents, whose attitudes and actions lie far beyond her reach.

7

$\mathcal{J}$ed and Nancy—
Loss Resulting from a
Sibling Rift

In our society, it's common for siblings to move apart geographically, and it's not unusual for other kinds of distances to grow between brothers and sisters. Sometimes, however, the distances are greater and more sudden than siblings anticipated—a consequence of family politics, envy, rivalry, or misunderstanding—and the results become a source of regret and resentment rather than being accepted.

This story focuses on a rift between Jed and Nancy Arieti, who are brother and sister, a rift that started around the time of their mother's diagnosis of cancer. The Arietis were a large family—three sons and three daughters. The father, Frank, had died many years before. Five out of six Arieti children remained in their hometown following their graduation from college; the sixth, Jed, had moved to Pennsylvania. Even that act of departure prompted the others to see Jed as the black sheep of the family. The tacit assumption among the Arieti kids had been that they would always be together, running the family automotive dealership and helping Mom. So in his siblings' eyes, Jed had betrayed the family even before their mother took ill.

The situation deteriorated further once her illness began. Mom had never been healthy, and when she was diagnosed with ovarian cancer at age sixty-eight, her condition deteriorated quickly. Yet a new form of chemotherapy made a remission possible. Everyone was pleased—she'd always been a real fighter—and she clearly wanted to live. The catch was that Mom required round-the-clock nursing care. Predictably, all of the Arieti kids pitched in.

Because the other five siblings lived in town, they could take care of Mom without disrupting their schedules. They shared the burden; each son or daughter took shifts looking after Mom. Jed, however, faced a different situation. He lived about five hours away, and he had his own car dealership to run. Jed didn't want to leave his siblings in the lurch, however, so he offered to compensate them for their more protracted time with Mom by footing the bill for a disproportionate share of medical bills, living expenses, and whatever else the family needed. His brothers and sisters generally agreed to his offers. Behind his back, though, some of them—including Nancy—felt that Jed had gotten "off the hook." A lot of resentment bubbled up around the issue of Jed's absence.

I should offer some background about this family. Before his death, Frank Arieti had had a serious drinking problem, and although he had always provided for his family, he had been emotionally absent. Mom Arieti had consequently looked to her children for her emotional sustenance and support. The Arietis did, in fact, work together as a family, but not without cost: a lot of the anger they felt toward their father's emotional absence eventually got displaced onto Jed, who they felt on some level was as unavailable as Frank had been.

In addition, the Arietis had an intense but somewhat inverted view of the family's purpose: they each saw their purpose as serving to support the family, rather than seeing the family's purpose as serving to support the individuals in the family. The situation was complex and, as family therapists would term it, *enmeshed*—they were intensely dependent on one another. Under these circumstances, it's not surprising that the one child who had found the courage to break away was precisely the one that the family scapegoated.

Mom Arieti compounded this situation in several ways. She was definitely a matriarch—a strong, powerful, loving mother—the sort of parent who provided most of the gravitational field that kept the family together. Once she died, that gravity dissipated. These were adult children; they could have reached their own insights about the family dynamics and made their own decisions about how to deal with them. Instead, Mom's death became a "green light" for the Arieti kids to vent the anger that they had repressed over the years. Their parents, being from the old school, had always been categorical about family behavior: "Be nice to your brother; be nice to your sister." Yet over all those years, the feelings that these siblings had been having toward each other—like many of the feelings that all siblings have—weren't particularly nice. And much of the anger was displaced onto Jed, who had chosen to leave home and become independent.

The situation was especially intense between Jed and Nancy. When Mom died, Nancy, the daughter who had always been most attached to her mother, felt even more furious than the others—angry, disenchanted, and abandoned. Interestingly, Nancy had been the most emotionally close to Jed when they'd been growing up; he had taken the place of her emotionally absent father in some respects. Therefore, it's understandable that she missed Jed the most and felt his absence most profoundly. Perhaps she felt that Jed was the sibling safest to "act out" on, because he was the one whom she trusted most. At the same time, there's no question that Nancy really did feel a tremendous amount of rage and disappointment at what she perceived to be the emotional abandonment resulting from her father's and mother's deaths.

Nancy and Jed are still almost entirely out of touch. The other siblings have tried to get them back together on numerous occasions, but without success. Jed and Nancy see each other at family parties and other occasions, and they're superficially cordial, but there's no real interaction between them. This is a sad situation for both. They miss each other. They want to be part of each other's lives. Unfortunately, they still haven't found a way to reach past their pain to connect once again.

This situation resembles Karen Larsson's in some respects, for Nancy and Jed have a choice: either cling to their mutual resentment and recriminations or else open their minds and hearts to each other. As with Karen's family, it's hard to predict what the Arietis will choose. The siblings' efforts to mend the bridges seem encouraging, though less so after several failures than before. Still, it's possible that future events will prompt a reconciliation between Jed and Nancy.

What concerns me about the Arietis' conflict that wasn't an issue in the Larssons' is the family's general, long-standing perception of Jed as the official outcast. The Arietis tended to be so collectively obsessed with loyalty (and loyalty narrowly defined) that they have considered Jed's independence deviant, even treasonous. This leaves Jed's siblings, especially Nancy, with a distorted frame of reference for perceiving their brother. Meanwhile, it leaves Jed backed into an uncomfortable corner. Until the Arietis grieve their losses—especially the loss of their mother, whose illness and death still suffuses the sibling conflicts—it's hard to believe that Jed and Nancy will focus on the present rather than staying bogged down in the past.

This issue of their focusing on the past is potentially a problem in its own right. Focusing on the past diminishes the Arietis' anxiety about present-day grief and helps them avoid the reality of their mother's death. By staying fixated on the past, the Arietis can pretend (at least to some extent) that their mother isn't really gone. This state of mind prolongs the inevitable pain of the grief process. Although anger is a common and often normal part of grief, the situation in the Arieti family may prompt its members to stay "stuck" in anger, because "it's easier to be mad than sad." One of the chief tasks facing the Arietis, both individually and collectively, is to put down their guard and start to feel the full range of their feelings of loss.

8

Lucinda and Jack—Loss of Access to Children Following a Divorce

Many people find that the most traumatic consequence of a divorce isn't the loss of a spouse, but the loss of contact (or reduction of contact) with children. Even a relatively amicable divorce means that one or both spouses will spend less time with their kids. A hostile divorce may well create a situation in which one parent ends up losing visitation rights altogether. The result is a tragedy for everyone concerned.

At an early age—she was eighteen and he was twenty—Lucinda and Jack got married. Neither set of parents felt entirely enthusiastic about this marriage, yet they weren't entirely against it, either. The couple's parents had married early, too, and both families felt pleased that Jack and Lucinda were at least marrying by choice, not by necessity. On the negative side, the parents went along with the couple's plans partly because the marriage all but guaranteed that the kids would leave home, which served the parents' own agendas. In addition, Lucinda had a history of intermittent clinical depression, and her parents hoped that marriage would (in their words) "give her a boost."

Lucinda, pregnant within a few months of marrying Jack, suffered a miscarriage. A year later she conceived again, however, and delivered a healthy son, whom the couple named Bruce. She was twenty at the time; Jack was twenty-two. Despite her initial relief about her son's birth, Lucinda soon experienced a major depression—probably a mixture of the chronic depressive states she had struggled with for years combined with the postpartum blues that affect many women following childbirth. Lucinda ended up undergoing psychotherapy and receiving antidepressant medications to counter this depression, and within a few months she started feeling better. She looked after Bruce full-time for a year, then resumed her job as a swing-shift data entry clerk. Jack, meanwhile, worked by day and spent his evenings with Bruce. Life seemed to stabilize.

Predictably, however, married life and parenthood proved strenuous for this young couple. Money was tight. Caring for Bruce seemed much harder than either spouse had expected. Lucinda worried that Jack would hold her recent depression against her, especially since his parents had always been suspicious of her stability. She was intent on making things work out, however, regardless of what was required. She worried that Jack seemed restless—bored, unhappy, stressed—but she wasn't sure what to do other than keep plugging away at the many tasks facing her. The truth was that Jack, though somewhat older than Lucinda, was far less mature, and despite Lucinda's struggle with depression, he was much more emotionally unstable.

One day, having gone home right after work, Lucinda discovered that the apartment was empty. Jack had cleaned the place out and left, taking Bruce with him. Lucinda felt shocked and incredulous—it simply wasn't possible. Burglars must have broken in and kidnapped Jack and the baby. Or else Jack's parents, having always disapproved of Lucinda, had talked their son into leaving. Lucinda couldn't believe that her husband had abandoned her.

She learned within a few days that Jack had fled cross-country with the child. It took her weeks to locate him and reestablish contact. When she succeeded, it turned out that her worst fears were well grounded: Jack's parents had conspired with him to "save" Bruce from Lucinda. They had convinced him that she wasn't fit for motherhood and that the baby would be better off separated from her. Jack refused Lucinda's entreaties to return. He intended to start a new life alone. Nothing she could do would change his mind.

Over the next eighteen years, Jack divorced Lucinda, married another woman, and raised another child with her. Lucinda never felt convinced that he was happy with his second wife, but her efforts to regain him never succeeded. This in itself became a great source of grief. What troubled and saddened her even more, though, was losing her son. With his parents' help, Jack managed to navigate the legal system; labeling Lucinda an unfit mother because of her psychiatric history, Jack gained full custody of Bruce. Lucinda saw her son just occasionally, most often at Christmas, at spring break, and for a couple of weeks in the summer. Even these visits occurred only after a protracted custody struggle. Lucinda eventually regained more consistent contact with Bruce, but she still missed out on much of the boy's early development. Later, as he grew older, Bruce started creating his own life—finding friends and developing interests—and he didn't feel as eager to see his mom each summer. Lucinda's initial victory in regaining visitation rights ended up seeming inadequate, even hollow.

In this way Lucinda suffered a kind of double divorce: not only had her husband abandoned her, but he had also engineered the aftermath of their marital divorce by limiting Lucinda's connection with her son in normal, day-to-day events. Bruce, raised by his father and hearing many hostile remarks and distorted bits of information about Lucinda, felt resentful and angry toward his mother. Lucinda gradually understood what was happening, and she felt tempted to retaliate. She usually held off, however, feeling that retaliation would only compound the problems she faced.

Lucinda eventually remarried. She now has a daughter by her second husband. She is happier than before and feels intent on "doing things right" the second time around. She also feels that her patience with Jack has paid off to some degree; she has gradually gained more time with Bruce. The mother-son rift has healed somewhat. Lucinda and Bruce are cordial toward one another. At the same time, Lucinda finds their relationship formal and stiff, nothing like the bond she'd hoped for and anticipated with her son. Lucinda continues to keep the door to communication open, and she tries not to take Bruce's indifference too personally; at the same time, she feels intense pain when Bruce rejects her overtures to connect with him.

I can't pretend that this story can have a happily-ever-after ending. Though believing himself well intentioned, Jack severely damaged his wife's and his son's lives. It would be irresponsible to pretend that anything can undo all the harm that these actions have created.

Still, Lucinda has several choices that can either ease her suffering to some degree or, on the other hand, intensify her pain. Facing her sense of loss directly allows at least the potential for coming to terms with grief and its consequences. The task is hard, but accepting it can lead to insight, growth, and some degree of consolation. Ignoring her loss, however—refusing to acknowledge or deal with it—could easily compound Lucinda's suffering. She can't undo the harmful acts that her ex-husband committed in the past, but she can prevent them from becoming depth charges that continue to detonate far into the future. She can't change her son's perception of her, but she can change her perception of herself, which in the long run may affect how Bruce sees and feels about his mother. Most of all, she can take better control of her life so that a tragic past doesn't poison her ability to enjoy the present, including the closeness she shares with her husband and daughter.

9

*M*ariella and Her Granddaughter—Loss of Access to Grandchildren Following a Divorce

Parents aren't the only ones who, in the aftermath of a divorce, may lose contact with children; it's not uncommon for grandparents to suffer a loss, too. Our society tends not to recognize the impact of this event. Although we often sentimentalize the bond between grandparents and grandkids, we don't generally acknowledge the depth of loss that both the older and younger generations may feel when this bond is severed.

Mariella had felt uneasy about her son's marriage for many years. Craig and his wife, Brynn, had seemed happy for a while, but their relationship soured at about the same time that Brynn gave birth to the couple's daughter, Sally. Brynn left Craig when Sally was just two years old. This situation confirmed Mariella's long-standing fears.

In some respects, the collapse of Craig's marriage was even worse than Mariella had expected. It appeared that Craig himself had caused the initial problem by indulging in a one-night stand with another woman. Brynn was furious. It was bad enough that he'd betrayed Brynn—but to do so within months of her giving birth! Mariella wasn't entirely sure of what had taken place, but she felt embarrassed and chagrined that her son might have done what

Brynn claimed. At the same time, she wanted to stay loyal to Craig and supportive of the young couple. And she felt reassured at least that Craig was contrite and willing to work things out.

Brynn would hear nothing of it. The marriage was over. She rejected Craig's offer to stay in close touch even though they had separated; she wanted nothing to do with him. To make matters worse, Brynn decided to leave town. Taking Sally with her, she broke off all but the most limited contact with Craig and his family. Brynn eventually took out her anger not just on her ex-husband but on her ex-in-laws as well. "I've had it with the whole bunch of you," she wrote in a rambling letter to Mariella. "I don't want to see any of you ever again. I don't want my little girl to see you either. None of you. And if you ever try coming near Sally you'll regret it. You'll never even know what hit you." Mariella couldn't believe the words she read. It wasn't that Mariella denied Brynn the right to feel hurt or angry; neither did Mariella doubt that Brynn loved her daughter. But how deep was Brynn's love, really, if she denied the girl the opportunity to spend time with her own grandparents?

At first, Mariella accepted her ex-daughter-in-law's decision, and she took seriously the implicit threat accompanying it. She didn't want to make matters worse. Perhaps Brynn would settle down after a while. Perhaps Craig would work out some sort of visitation arrangement—an arrangement that might give Mariella access to Sally, too. But as the months passed, Mariella grew more concerned and angry. Did it make sense, she wondered, to go along with Brynn's preferences so passively? Was it really certain that this bitter woman would retaliate simply because Mariella wanted to share in a relationship that most grandparents took for granted? Or did it make sense to gamble, assert herself, and take a stand? About a year after her son's separation from his wife, Mariella took Brynn to court, demanding visitation rights.

The battle over Sally lasted almost two years. In theory, Mariella won: she gained access to her granddaughter for two days each month. In practice, though, the situation is more complex. Brynn often calls on the scheduled visitation days to announce that Sally is sick or otherwise unavailable. Sometimes Brynn simply isn't at home when Mariella arrives to pick up Sally. Winning the battle isn't winning the war. And even when Mariella works things out with Brynn and spends some time with Sally, it's not without having paid a great cost: Mariella hadn't been able to see Sally until the child was almost four years old. There's always an ache when she realizes how much of her granddaughter's development she has already missed.

Mariella's loss obviously resembles Lucinda's (described in the previous story) in many respects. The main difference—a significant complicating factor for Mariella—is that grandparents have far fewer legal options than parents do in demanding visitation rights. Mariella has, in fact, succeeded far better than many grandparents in gaining access to her grandchild. There are complicating factors, though. One is that Brynn's evasiveness in fulfilling her obligations leaves Mariella largely without recourse. The courts, swamped by other custody and visitation cases, are unlikely to reprimand Brynn for noncompliance with the grandparental agreement. Another complicating factor is that contemporary society pays relatively little attention to Mariella's type of loss. Americans acknowledge the importance of grandparents to some degree; however, Mariella finds that only other grandparents understand the depth of her frustration, anger, and sadness. As a result, Mariella grieves mostly in solitude for the time she has lost with Sally.

The African proverb "It takes a whole village to raise one child" brings home the point that children need the input of many different people in their lives to develop their full potential. Lack of contact with grandparents cuts children off from the special kinds of love, attention, and pride that only grandparents can provide. It also deprives children of a sense of history, cultural beliefs, values, and activities that give them a richer, deeper sense of where their ancestors originated and where their potential can take them. Grandparents are the historians who pass on the family heritage to the next generation.

Brynn's efforts to sever the grandparent-grandchild bond clearly interrupt and damage the natural flow of information from one generation to the next, and it removes an essential opportunity for Sally to feel loved and to learn more about herself and her place in the family. Sally and Mariella are obviously the big losers in this regard. Ironically, Brynn suffers a loss, too: whatever deprives a child of depth and fulfillment ultimately deprives the parent of something, whether the parent perceives the loss or not.

10

Carrie, Carl, and Their Friends—Loss of Friends Following a Divorce

When a couple goes through the ordeal of divorce, both partners tend to focus initially on their own relationship. Their anger, grief, and sadness most intensely affect themselves and each other. At some point, however—perhaps early on, perhaps later—the consequences of the divorce start affecting other relationships. Most divorcing partners eventually cease to interact as often (if at all) with their in-laws. This may or may not be agreeable to the divorcing couple. Some people delight in "being rid" of their in-laws; others may regret the loss of these relatives.

What most divorcing partners don't anticipate is the loss of *friends*. A divorce affects not just family relationships but friendships as well. This ripple effect, the severing of one set of ties creating tensions or hard feelings that sever still other ties, may come as a terrible shock. And this shock in turn can intensify the sense of loss that the divorcing partners feel.

When Carrie and Carl Salvatore chose to get divorced, their friends tried to maintain a sense of balance with the couple. The Salvatores had enjoyed a wide circle of friends—some from school days, others from the couple's married life together. Carl had gone to school with many of the men. Carrie had her own group of friends, too, both from childhood and later years. As members of this social group got married over the years, the circle had continually expanded.

Divorce often creates fault lines within a couple's social group, and this situation certainly held true for Carl and Carrie. The friends took sides according to who was the original friend of whom. Carl's male friends, especially, were quick to ally themselves with their old pal; most of them ceased contact with Carrie at the outset. Carrie felt that these men may have felt pressures from Carl to show their loyalty ("You're either her friend or mine, but not both of ours"), and she felt profoundly uncomfortable in their presence. Carrie's friends, meanwhile, maintained their alliance with her and generally ceased contact with Carl. None of this particularly surprised Carrie. The situation saddened her, though: although she had friends of her own, she regretted the loss of Carl's longtime friends, since she had been part of the same school group and had known all these people for years. She also felt shocked by their behavior, since she had somehow imagined that when she and Carl separated, their friends would maintain their connection to both partners.

The situation created many hard feelings at an already painful time. It wasn't just that these friends backed off from Carrie; the worst aspect was the hurtful, foolish things that people said. There were excuses: "You have a better family than Carl does" or "We feel sorrier for him than for you" or "He doesn't have as many friends as you do" or "We like you, but we don't like your new boyfriend." What did all those words *mean*? Carrie didn't know. One way or another, from the day that she and Carl first separated, most of the couple's friends stopped calling Carrie. Except for her own longtime friends, none of these people asked her out, invited her for dinner, or even called to keep in touch with her. Carrie felt that in their eyes, she had simply disappeared.

What had happened? It took Carrie months to figure it out. First of all, there was the reality of Carrie's anger and grief. She *was* angry and grief-stricken. Carl had left Carrie for another woman, so why shouldn't she feel angry? But as time passed, Carrie realized how threatening her rage and depression must have been to some of these old friends. It hit too close to home. They couldn't tolerate her pain. It wasn't just that they felt uncomfortable with Carrie's own grief; her grief also hinted at the losses that these people, too, might suffer some day. *They* could have been the couple suffering a bitter divorce. Their conflicts from their own families and histories and their insecurities and denial about their own marriages had been transferred to their relationship with Carrie and Carl.

Carrie could admit to herself that Carl was an easier person to hang out with. He wasn't emotive, he didn't share his feelings, and he wasn't communicative or expressive. In addition, he was a good pal—a fun guy to have around, another player on the basketball court, a good partner for a tennis match. He served a purpose that was more beneficial than Carrie's for this group of friends. Ironically, Carrie had been much more giving in the couple's relationship with these friends; Carl was more distant. This worked to his advantage, however, since most of these people didn't *want* expression. They wanted fun. And Carrie, being more expressive about her pain, became intolerable to these people, who felt committed mostly to establishing their careers and having their families. They were all in their mid-thirties to early forties. They really weren't interested in nurturing a friend in need at that time. They were self-absorbed with their own lives.

In addition, Carrie's status as a newly single woman created tension within the group. Some of the men felt threatened by the thought of their wives hanging out with a single woman—someone who knew a lot of their secrets and who wasn't constrained now by an affiliation with her husband. If divorce could hit the Salvatores, perhaps this misfortune could strike these other couples, too. And some of the women, meanwhile, felt equally uncomfortable with

Carrie's unattached status. Here was a young, attractive, and now-single woman. . . . What sort of trouble could she make among their husbands? Most of these couples couldn't handle the stress.

As a consequence of their divorce, Carrie and Carl suffered multiple losses. Each lost the other as a spouse—a loss they hadn't anticipated but ultimately chose and considered necessary. This loss was the most severe of those they experienced. The loss of in-laws, too, created its own sadness and frustration, since both Carl and Carrie had grown close to some of their relatives by marriage. In some ways what surprised and confused them more than these other losses, however, was the loss of friends. They lost not only each other but also an entire social circle. This continues to affect Carrie more than Carl. Aloof and easygoing, Carl took his loss in stride. For Carrie, however, the loss of so many friends was a huge setback precisely at a time when she needed as much emotional support as possible.

Here again is a situation that seems unjust and undeserved. In Carrie's situation, however, the loss of these relationships doesn't seem a concerted act by Carl—something he forced on her—so much as a cluster of betrayals by individual friends. Carrie doesn't even know whom to blame. Maybe there's no one to blame at all; what happened just happened. The catch is that Carrie still acutely grieves the loss of her friends, and she still has to face the consequences of their absence from her life. She feels some consolation from realizing that some of these friends abandoned her as a consequence of their own self-absorption and immaturity; if they had been more mature, they might well have maintained a degree of detachment from the divorcing couple's crisis. Early on following the divorce, however, this sort of realization provided only limited solace.

What should she do? There's no easy answer to that question. Some marriages create such a powerful gravitational field that friendships, like planets attracted by a star, end up pulled into orbit around the couple. Carrie and Carl had such a marriage. Now, following their divorce, the gravitational force has diminished; the dynamic has changed. It's almost inevitable that each former spouse must reconstruct a social life different from what he or she experienced before. Most people succeed at this task, though some more quickly than others. What compounds their problem is that, as already noted, the experience of divorce usually brings a cluster of losses—loss of spouse, loss of in-laws, loss of friends, and sometimes loss of children. Dealing with any loss is difficult. Dealing with several at once is more so. What we'll soon discuss, however, is that all losses have more common elements than differences and that dealing with one may allow access to dealing with another.

PART III

*M*ending a Broken Heart

*T*he loss of a spouse or partner; the loss of a parent, child, or other relative; the loss of friends—all of these losses are significant, powerful, and potentially hurtful. If you've experienced these or other losses, you may find yourself confused, troubled, hurt, even emotionally paralyzed by the impact of what's happened. Simultaneously, friends and family members may be telling you, "Pull yourself together," "Get on with life," or "Don't wallow in emotions." These comments are perfectly well intentioned—and often perfectly useless. How can you pull yourself together when you feel as if you've been dashed to bits? How can you get on with life when it seems to have ended? How can you avoid wallowing in emotions when, despite your best efforts, you feel as if you're drowning in sadness, confusion, or rage?

I've sketched a variety of losses in the preceding chapters. My purpose has been primarily to show the commonality of what people experience when brokenhearted and how intensely many men and women feel their sense of loss. The rest of *How to Mend a Broken Heart* focuses on what you can do to understand your loss, face it, come to terms with it, and move on to the rest of your life, all by means of the following six-step process:

Step 1: Understanding the Nature of Loss

Step 2: Focusing on the Self

Step 3: Dealing with the Shadow Side

Step 4: Stabilizing Your Life

Step 5: Becoming Aware of Your Recovery

Step 6: Accepting Progress, Not Perfection

The sections that follow describe these steps and what they involve.

Understanding the Nature of Loss

The stories in Part II provide a sense of what you may experience after a relationship ends. Intense, complex, even contradictory emotions are common; difficult practical problems can occur; and you may perceive changes in how you see yourself and others.

To some extent, these consequences may follow any loss of a close relationship. All losses resemble each other in some respects. What hits hard under almost all circumstances is that a bond of great personal significance has ended and that loss now affects you. You feel confused, angry, frustrated, in pain, or all of these emotions simultaneously. You feel physically and emotionally exhausted. You can't imagine how you'll go on, yet you still have obligations and expectations. How can you go on—yet how can you *not* go on?

Before considering the ways in which you can let go of your past relationship and move on with your life, however, consider one of the most important aspects of dealing with loss: the nature of bereavement and grief.

What Are Bereavement and Grief?

"Bereavement is the reaction to the loss of a close relationship," according to Beverley Raphael, an Australian psychiatrist whose book *The Anatomy of Bereavement* is one of the best on the subject. Dr. Raphael and other experts believe that this reaction is one that human beings undergo to help them adapt to loss. If two people have a significant relationship and that relationship ends, bereavement of some sort is a likely consequence. Dr. Raphael's work has often focused on bereavement following loss through death; however, her comments on this subject hold true for other kinds of loss as well. The sense of loss you experience following a divorce or other breakup, for instance, may well resemble what you would experience following a loved one's death. The more significant the relationship, the more likely it is that bereavement will be intense. Bereavement is in some respects the cost of emotional commitment.

Although bereavement is a reaction, what follows it is a process. This process involves a variety of emotions—sadness, longing, bewilderment, and so forth—collectively referred to as *grief.* Bereavement and grief are potentially confusing concepts. The main point to remember is that these experiences are all part of a process. When a significant relationship has ended, you need time to adjust to the loss. The grief process doesn't happen all at once. It occurs over a period of time, often a longer time than you may find comfortable. It can't be rushed or compressed. The grief process, though painful in many ways, has its own internal logic; if allowed to proceed, it almost always resolves successfully.

There are two aspects of this situation that we should consider. One is that the bereavement and grief are normal. The other is that bereavement and grief, being part of a process, have phases to their development.

The Normality of Bereavement and Grief

For centuries, some people have tended to regard grief as a kind of illness. Even now you may sometimes hear people speak of someone being "sick with grief" or "dying of grief." There is some truth to these perceptions. As Colin Murray Parkes and Robert S. Weiss (respectively an English psychiatrist and an American sociologist) have noted in their book *Recovery from Bereavement*: "After all, grief is a very painful condition that impairs the ability of the afflicted individual to function effectively in everyday activities. It produces a range of somatic symptoms: heaviness in the limbs, sighing, restless apathy, loss of appetite and weight, sleeplessness and languor, with pangs of acute distress."

At the same time, these perceptions of grief as an illness miss an important dimension to what happens during the grief process. Dr. Parkes and Dr. Weiss go on: "Yet there are also grounds for regarding grief as the 'normal' accompaniment of a major loss. . . . We see grief as a normal reaction to overwhelming loss, albeit a reaction in which normal functioning no longer holds." A good comparison might be your body's response to a broken leg. The damage to the bone is clearly harmful. You are in pain. If you ignore the injury or expect it to heal overnight, you may do yourself much worse damage than what you have already suffered. But if you let your body's capacity for self-healing do its work, then you will recover. The broken bone may even end up stronger than it was before breaking.

The grief process is more complicated than the healing of broken bones, of course, and subtler as well. But the basic analogy is appropriate. Bereavement is the human organism's adjustment to major loss. This adjustment, as well as the grief you feel as part of it, is a sign of health—not a sign of dysfunction. Bereavement and grief are normal.

The Individuality of Bereavement and Grief

The grief process is highly individual. There is no reason why your experience should necessarily resemble what someone else goes through. After all, your relationship with your loved one was unique; when the relationship ends, your sense of loss, too, will be unique.

"Everybody comes into the situation of bereavement bringing a whole history," according to Anne Rosberger, a therapist at the Bereavement and Loss Center in New York City. "It's not as if they just came to this point and it's all entirely new. Every time you have a loss of any kind, other feelings around separation begin to surface. So you are bringing with it a lot of your past experience." The personal background of loss partially accounts for the individuality of grief reactions.

For this reason, you should remember that you don't owe anyone any particular emotion, expression, set of words, or gestures during the course of your grief process. If people around you imply that you seem insufficiently affected—perhaps you're not "upset enough" about the relationship that has ended—then their reaction has more to do with their own expectations than with your feelings. The same is true if you get the message that you're too emotional, too upset, or too sad, or if anyone suggests that you are too giddy, too spacey, too nostalgic. Wendy Foster-Evans, a counselor in Marin County, California, believes that "people need to go through the grief process at their own pace and in their own way. Some people are very private about grief; others are really expressive. Either way, that's to be honored."

No one can decide what your relationship with someone else has meant to you; the same holds true for the loss of that relationship and the person you loved.

Bereavement, Grief, and Emotions

The grief process usually includes intense emotions. The particular emotions, their intensity, and their duration vary from one person to another. Likely as not, however, you will experience some sort of grief—some sort of emotional reaction to the loss of a close relationship and to the changes that this loss creates in your life. Since these feelings are often surprising—either stronger, weaker, or different from what you might have expected—I will sketch the range of possibilities.

Shock

One of the most common emotions right after a loss is shock. This emotion is especially common if the loss occurs without warning, but you may feel a sense of shock even if you knew in advance that your relationship would end. No matter how aware you might have been in advance, you're never entirely prepared for the death of someone you love.

Dr. Raphael says that during a state of shock, "The bereaved person feels a sense of unreality, as though . . . it must be happening to someone else. The bereaved may feel distance from the horror and its implications, frozen in time. There is a feeling of being in a dream or a nightmare from which he will awake." You may find it hard to believe that someone could be so fully present in your life one moment and gone the next or that the delight and affection that you shared with your loved one could turn into anger and retribution. The collapse of a relationship seems a strange, incomprehensible event.

Here's an example. When he was twenty-two years old, Ted fell in love with Beth, a college friend who had moved to Ted's city in search of employment. Ted and Beth began a delightful, almost idyllic relationship and soon decided to share an apartment together. Neither had ever experienced such happiness with another person. Ted felt sure that he wanted to marry Beth, and he proposed to her a few months later. Beth quickly accepted, intensifying the couple's happiness.

During a Christmas vacation visit to Beth's parents' house out of state, however, a complication arose: Ted's future in-laws, though outwardly cordial, seemed cool to the notion of the marriage. Cultural differences between the two families prompted Beth's parents to feel that their daughter shouldn't marry Ted. The visit proceeded. Ted and Beth discussed the situation earnestly, and Ted felt confident of his ability to sort things out with his fiancée. Then Ted finished his Christmas visit and went alone to his own hometown. He strongly believed that his love for Beth and Beth's for him would triumph over any parental objections.

Beth called Ted just a week later. In light of her parents' reservations about Ted, she had decided to break off their engagement. In addition, she had concluded that on her return to Ted's city, she would move out of the apartment they shared and ultimately end the relationship. Ted felt profound shock at this news. First of all, he hadn't expected this turn of events. Second, he experienced a tremendous sense of loss at Beth's decision. Third, he felt astonished that Beth could capitulate so quickly and so totally to her parents' pressure—a capitulation that cast a shadow over their previous year's time together and the delight that Ted had experienced in Beth's company. Although Ted recovered his emotional equilibrium within a few weeks, he wasn't prepared for the shock he felt after breaking up with his lover.

Shock is generally an emotion that fades within a few days or weeks. For some people, though, it can be remarkably durable. If your loss has occurred suddenly (such as if you feel jilted by someone who has abruptly disappeared from your life), you may find it difficult to believe that the loss has happened at all. You may find yourself mistaking a stranger's voice for your loved one's, or you may catch sight of someone you imagine to be that person. These perceptual tricks are disturbing. You may worry that you're hallucinating or even going crazy. However, many people experience these tricks of the mind. They are merely a side effect of shock and almost always are harmless. Once your mind has had a while to adjust to a sudden and confusing change, the sense of shock and its effects will diminish.

Sadness and Depression

When a significant relationship ends, you may experience sadness, depression, or both. The difference between these two reactions is important but often not recognized in our culture. Both reactions are common expressions of bereavement.

John Bowlby, the English psychiatrist whose studies of bereavement and grief form the basis of much research on the subject, states in his book *Loss* that "sadness is a normal and healthy response to any misfortune. Most, if not all, more intense episodes of sadness are elicited by the loss, or expected loss, either of a loved person or else of family. . . ." Sadness during the grief process is essentially an emotional response to the finitude of human life or of certain experiences. It is a recognition that something important is over; someone who once filled a significant place in your life is now gone.

Sadness may affect you in general ways, as it affected Janice. She had carried on a yearlong love relationship with Sam, who had always seemed as smitten with her as she was with him. Janice assumed that they would eventually get married and settle down together. When Sam announced abruptly "I'm not ready to commit myself" and moved suddenly to the West Coast, Janice felt many emotions, among them great sadness. What had seemed a strong bond simply vanished overnight. It wasn't surprising or inappropriate for Janice to feel sad in response to this sudden loss. The sadness that Janice felt is predictable given her close relationship with Sam and the frustrating way that the relationship ended.

Yet sometimes sadness comes as a surprise. If your relationship had showed signs of severe stress or if you had reached a point of not wanting it to continue, you may tend to assume that its absence from your life won't sadden you when the relationship ends. Especially in acrimonious or abusive relationships, the partners may actually desire dissolution. But sadness is usually part of the grief process anyway; it's part of the partners' regret over what the relationship used to be or could have been.

For instance, Pedro and Aline lived together for almost three years before they decided that their arrangement simply wasn't worth the effort. They believed their relationship was a mistake; although they had been in love during their first year together, their emotions toward one another eventually shifted until annoyance and resentment predominated. They stayed together from force of habit, not delight, passion, or mutual respect. In some ways their breakup was long overdue. Once they separated, however, both partners felt a tremendous sense of sadness. Why couldn't things have been better? How could two fundamentally generous, good-hearted people have spent such a long time arguing and causing each other problems? And (perhaps this above all) why had they taken so long to see the light? Even though Pedro and Aline were right to part company, the separation still created a sense of sadness.

Depression resembles sadness in some respects but differs significantly from it in other ways. Dr. Bowlby regards depression as a mood that is "an inevitable accompaniment of any state in which behavior becomes disorganized, as it is likely to do after a loss." Depression is a way in which your mind distances itself from disruptive changes in your life and allows you time to reorganize. Depression, however, often seems less an emotion than an *absence* of emotion. It frequently resembles a kind of fatigue.

Many people become depressed following a major loss. This kind of emotional response to a loss isn't at all unusual. What is most important to remember about both sadness and depression is that *not only are they normal, but they almost always diminish with the passage of time.* Sadness and depression are part of the complicated adjustment you are making to loss. Although many people feel acutely sad or depressed following the loss of a significant relationship, few end up being overwhelmed by their emotions. Almost all bereaved men and women find that their sadness and depression ease after a while, and that the pain they feel gradually gives way to more comfortable emotions. (Lingering depression, however, is a potentially worrisome experience. We will examine it and what to do about it later in this book.)

Relief

Compared with predictable emotions like shock and sadness, relief often worries many people following a loss. You may end up asking yourself, for instance, how you can feel relieved that an important relationship has ended. Consider, for example, how our culture idealizes marriage. Couples may feel great pressure to stay married even when the relationship has deteriorated severely; as a result, one or both spouses may feel that dissolving the marriage indicates a complete failure and that he or she has no right to be relieved that it's over. Yet the dissolution of the marriage may be cause for genuine relief. Let's say that you've given your marriage your best efforts but find that the relationship can't (for whatever reasons) continue. Why shouldn't you feel relieved that far from having "failed," you have simply taken the relationship and developed it as far as possible? And under other circumstances—such as a hostile, even destructive, relationship—why shouldn't you feel relieved that the conflict has ended? Shock, sadness, and other emotions complicate a sense of relief, but they don't contradict it.

Recall the story of Aline and Pedro, mentioned earlier. As noted, this couple felt deep sadness in breaking up, and this emotion was appropriate; at the same time, both partners felt a sense of relief to have finally ended a relationship that caused more ill feelings than good. They had faced reality at last. They had acted on the necessity of severing an unpleasant, counterproductive bond. And they were now both free to look elsewhere for love and fulfillment, which they each succeeded in finding with other partners within a few years' time.

Another example of unanticipated relief is what sometimes occurs following the loss of a job. Most people feel dismay, sadness, anxiety, and anger when fired or forced to resign from their place of employment. At the same time, many people feel a simultaneous sense of relief. The workplace may have been hostile or tense, the job itself may have ceased to be personally or professionally worthwhile, or the uncertainty over bureaucratic decisions may have become intolerable. In these and other situations, receiving the pink slip may inspire relief as well as concern or frustration.

There's nothing wrong with feeling relief under these and other circumstances. Although everyone wishes that relationships could be happy and supportive, reality often falls short of these expectations. Relief following the end of a difficult relationship is certainly appropriate. Similarly, it's not uncommon for people to respond to unemployment with mixed emotions.

Regret and Guilt
Perhaps you feel you should have done more for the person you loved; you should have been a better wife, husband, lover, parent, or friend; you should have said more, said less, said something other than what you ended up saying. After a major loss, any mistakes and errors of judgment made during the relationship can make you feel that you failed or fell short. According to Dr. Raphael's *The Anatomy of Bereavement,* "Regret over what has been lost, what cannot be achieved now . . . are common emotions." And, too, "Guilt is frequent: it relates to the imperfection of human relationships."

A good example is Martina. During her twenties, Martina fell in love with an older man and carried on a three-year affair with him. Pete was forty-two, married, and employed as a manager in the automotive supply company where Martina worked as a secretary. The affair was passionate and delightful in many ways—Martina's first experience with a relatively long-term relationship and a source of tremendous growth and self-knowledge. It turned unpleasant, however, when Pete grew skittish with Martina about his involvement when Pete's wife discovered the affair. The whole situation collapsed within a few days afterward. Martina rarely saw Pete after that, and Pete's marriage barely survived his infidelity. In response, Martina felt deep regret over her abrupt loss of a friend and lover; she also felt guilty over having contributed to the near destruction of a family. The situation ultimately stabilized, but Martina wrestled with her emotions for a long time thereafter.

Even a more satisfying relationship can produce regrets. The demands of involvement with another person—whether that person is a spouse, lover, child, grandchild, friend, or sibling—are potential sources of guilt. Few people emerge from the ordeal unscathed.

Marcia Lattanzi, a bereavement counselor in Boulder County, Colorado, summarizes the situation: "Guilt is a very prominent emotion in bereavement. It is usually expressed in the desire to have *done* more or to have *said* something different or better. In simple terms, it is a punishment of the self for seemingly not living up to one's expectations of oneself." Guilt is one of the most common reactions during the grief process.

But it's important to keep these issues in context. First, the *presence* of guilt feelings doesn't mean that you have *reason* to feel guilty. Guilt may simply be a side effect of ordinary human fallibility. It seems a common experience to love another person and end up feeling guilty when the relationship ends. You wanted to do more but couldn't—or at least you couldn't to the degree that you would have liked. And so the guilt and regret end up surfacing. These feelings may be subtle; they may be intense. But they are there.

Second, be aware that *the grief process intensifies most feelings.* As a consequence of your grief, you may be recalling missed opportunities and errors of judgment in ways that distort their real importance within your relationship. This isn't to say that shortcomings didn't exist and mistakes didn't occur; however, these shortcomings and mistakes may not have been as significant as you imagine. If you broke up with your lover, for instance, you may imagine that your having exerted more effort or spoken different words might have saved the relationship. It's certainly possible that greater efforts might have made a difference. More often, however, such beliefs about missed opportunities are little more than wishful thinking; grief has simply intensified your sense of what your actions can accomplish.

Guilt may also be a way of distracting yourself from the painful process of accepting loss and coping with grief. If you blame yourself for your part in the collapse of a relationship, you are to some extent empowering yourself with more control than you really possessed before your loss occurred. This state of mind can lead to the following sorts of thoughts: "If I caused the relationship to collapse, then maybe I have the power to save it or fix it" or "If I have the power to cause these problems, maybe I have the power to solve them." As noted in Part I, this line of reasoning is typical of children's magical thinking: "If Mom and Dad are angry at me, it must be my fault. And if I behave myself better, I'll win their love back." Such attitudes are understandable at certain phases of the grief process, but they often serve chiefly to delay your facing the reality of change.

Anger
Like guilt, anger is common following bereavement—though you may regard anger, like relief, as a forbidden emotion. Yet as Dr. Bowlby and other researchers have noted, many people feel some sort of anger in the aftermath of loss—anger at being abandoned; anger at being left with bills to pay, problems to solve, or children to raise; or anger at having expended so much effort on a relationship that ultimately ended.

Here's an example. Jamie (mentioned first in Part 1) gave birth to twin daughters while married to her first husband. When the marriage dissolved, the girls, Sophie and Sadie, were only one year old, and Jamie gained custody of her daughters without much trouble. During later years, however, Jamie's ex-husband, Herb, sued for custody and almost succeeded in gaining it. Herb claimed that Jamie was emotionally unstable, hence unfit to be the twins' custodial parent. In fact, Jamie *did* have significant emotional problems and had received psychiatric counseling for years. Yet she was a deeply committed parent, had struggled energetically to win the battle with her problems, and had never done anything that could be construed as detrimental to her daughters. And Herb, too, was psychologically troubled. The custody battle raged for many years. Time after time, Jamie succeeded in retaining control of the twins. She felt tremendous anger at her ex-husband, however, for augmenting her problems, damaging her public reputation, and costing her tens of thousands of dollars in legal expenses. Although she knew that her anger was justified, Jamie often felt appalled to feel such rage—a common reaction, especially among women living in a culture that regards anger as a "bad" emotion unsuitable for women.

You may also feel angry not just at your loved one but at others seemingly implicated in the relationship or its end. For instance, many people feel angry at their in-laws following a divorce. Even close relationships with your ex-spouse's family may dissolve into partisan bickering. The same often holds true for nonmarital bonds, including other love relationships, sibling ties, and friendships. There's often a high degree of "guilt by association" and consequent anger.

These are all understandable reactions. Anger may not be pretty or comfortable, but it's often understandable. Your loss put you under stress; demanded your time, attention, patience, or self-denial; and ultimately resulted in your losing someone of great significance in your life. Why shouldn't you be angry? What makes anger difficult is that it's often socially unacceptable to express what you feel toward the people or institutions you hold responsible—friends, family, or institutional figures (judges, social workers, counselors). Sometimes the object of your wrath—fate, God, or simply the nature of things—is beyond your reach.

Yet in some respects, anger is a predictable reaction to all these developments. Many people feel embarrassed or frightened by their anger. However, anger is a normal part of the grief process—an essential part of determining a sense of your own identity following a loss. Anger can put you in touch with what you truly feel, and it can help to protect you from further violations by others. (For example, a wife whose husband has taken advantage of her in one or more ways—sexually, financially, psychologically—may find that anger helps defend her from future exploitation.) Admittedly, anger can feel frightening, at times overwhelmingly so. But keep in mind that angry thoughts and feelings are destructive only if you take action on them, whether toward others or toward yourself. Most people do *not* act on their fantasies, however; most people are more inclined to repress angry feelings because they seem uncomfortable or "ugly." Such repression is a potential risk. Later sections of this book consider ways of dealing with anger. For the moment, it's worth noting that a counselor or therapist may be useful in sorting out different kinds of anger and anticipating their effects on your life.

Longing

You may find that you can accept your loss a short time after it occurs. However, you may also find that loss produces intense and sometimes protracted longing for your loved one. Like other emotions that surface during the bereavement process, longing can cause you to worry that something is amiss. But also like the other emotions, longing is a normal reaction to loss.

Since adults have many kinds of relationships, longing can take many forms. The most common is simply wistfulness for whatever had been good and supportive and enjoyable. Here is an example. Ted, noted earlier in this chapter, recovered quickly from the collapse of his relationship with Beth. He moved on with his life and eventually established other love bonds with women. For years after his separation from Beth, however, he thought about her and sometimes even longed for her. It's not that he wanted to return to that relationship; he felt more satisfied sharing his life with other people. Rather, his longing for Beth—strong at first, subtler with the passing years—was simply an acknowledgment that she had been and still was a good, loving person and that their time together had been important and satisfying in his own growth as a human being.

Perhaps you feel that longing for someone is inappropriate. As an adult, you are mature and independent. You may therefore feel that longing implies dependence. In fact, you can be a fully functioning adult—one who perhaps sustained your loved one more substantially than he or she sustained you—and still feel a sense of longing after loss. Longing isn't necessarily a sign of emotional reliance on someone else. Instead, it seems just as likely to indicate how deep the bond was with the person you loved and how long it lasted. It's an acknowledgment of how strong a tie can grow when people accept each other.

Which of these emotions you feel, when, and to what degree will depend on many circumstances. Some of these circumstances are a result of bereavement in general. That is, some are a result of the effects that you would feel following *any* loss. Others are more specific to whatever emotions follow the loss that you have experienced. Still others are unique to your own personality.

However, now that we've examined them separately, it's worth noting that these emotions don't usually occur one by one but in combinations. And they often (though not always) occur in a fairly predictable sequence.

The Phases of the Grief Process

During the past several decades, the social scientists who study bereavement and grief have identified several phases that people go through during the grief process. These phases make it easier to understand what formerly seemed a shapeless, confusing jumble of experiences.

The most persuasive theory of phases during the grief process is that formulated by Dr. Bowlby. Writing in *Loss,* one of the fundamental books on the subject, Dr. Bowlby states that people go through four phases of grieving after a loss. These phases are (1) numbing, (2) yearning and searching, (3) disorganization and despair, and (4) reorganization. Most people experience all of these phases in one way or another. However, as Dr. Bowlby emphasizes, "Admittedly these phases are not clear-cut, and any one individual may oscillate for a time back and forth between any two of them." This oscillation is an important aspect of bereavement. The grief process rarely proceeds in a smooth, even flow from one experience to another. Instead, it often involves a mixture of emotions—sometimes with considerable uncertainty and ambivalence along the way.

In addition, the nature of your relationship and the circumstances of the loss make a difference in what you experience during these phases. A sudden loss will affect you differently from a loss that you've anticipated. The loss of a spouse through divorce will affect you differently from the loss of a friendship through gradual "growing apart," which in turn will affect you differently from the loss of visitation rights to a child, and so forth. (This book will examine these various differences in later chapters.) But overall, as Dr. Bowlby explained in an interview, "I think this general scheme is applicable toward almost all experiences of bereavement. It is either much intensified in certain situations or very much modified and attenuated. But this overall pattern applies to all forms of bereavement experiences."

One other important consideration is that these emotions are often interrelated. They can intensify and even trigger each other. For instance, if your relationship deteriorated over a long period of time, your sadness over the long process may heighten a sense of guilt that you couldn't or didn't do more to help. Anger can in turn feed both sadness and guilt. The interactions can go on and on. The particular pattern of emotions varies from one person to another or even within one person from one time to another. Sometimes the interactions are difficult to follow, let alone to understand. The important thing is to be aware that the jumble of emotions is almost inevitable. And, too, it will subside.

If you have heard that grief occurs in a fixed set of stages, it's worth noting that social scientists have developed theories about the phases of the grief process as a theoretical tool, *not as a precise way of determining what any one person should or will feel following a loss.* The grief process has a certain order to it, but it progresses through what are actually overlapping, fluid phases. You will cause yourself undue worry if you expect your thoughts and feelings to follow a straightforward course during the grief process.

Duration of the Grief Process

How long do these emotions last? This question is difficult to answer. The duration of intense emotions during the grief process varies enormously depending on the loss. As Anne Rosberger of the Bereavement and Loss Center says, "Most people want to know 'How long am I going to feel this way?' When you're in pain, you want to know that there's an end point. You can tolerate a certain amount of anxiety and pain if you know that at such and such time, it'll all be over. I wish we had a crystal ball. But we don't. It really is so individually determined."

People show an enormous range of response. Some people feel strong emotions for only a few days or weeks. Others remain upset for months, even years. What you experience depends on your own personality, your state of physical and emotional health, your relationship, the circumstances of how it ended, your social support system, and other factors. Precisely because the interaction of these variables makes for enormously varied responses, you should keep in mind that there is no single "right" sequence of events. Normal responses range from those in which people feel little or no distress to those in which people feel bereaved for several years.

What you can assume is that whatever your particular emotions, the intensity of your grief reaction will probably let up gradually. In addition, these emotions tend to be recurrent. Even when you expect to feel no more anger, sadness, or regret, the feelings can well up again. Such recurrences, like the slow subsiding of emotions, are also normal. Grief is rarely something that you can be over and done with and never feel again. Yet, if allowed to run its course, the grief process almost always resolves itself satisfactorily.

There is no such thing as generic grief. Each kind of relationship produces a somewhat different sense: the aftermath of a divorce differs from the consequences of a sibling rift, which differs from the aftermath of friends' parting ways, which in turn differs from a grandmother's involuntary separation from her grandchildren. Even so, the grief process discussed so far applies in general to the aftermath of many relationships.

Where does this leave you? Once you understand the nature of loss, how should you cope with it?

This is the question I'll consider next.

What to Remember About Step 1: Understanding the Nature of Loss

▲ Grief and bereavement, though painful, are a normal response to loss (whether the loss is the result of death, divorce, being rejected, etc.).
▲ Grief and bereavement are highly individual experiences.
▲ The grief process includes intense emotions.

▲ Typically, these emotions include shock, sadness and depression, relief, regret and guilt, anger, and longing.

▲ The grief process often follows fairly predictable phases, but these phases don't necessarily occur as precise, sequential stages.

▲ Grief varies in duration; some people experience a relatively brief grief process, while others grieve a relatively longer period of time.

$\mathcal{F}$ocusing on the Self

Once you've gained a better understanding of loss, you proceed to Step 2, "Focusing on the Self." This step is necessary before you can let go and move on with your life. The reason is that when you suffer a significant loss, your self-esteem is generally low. You may feel unresolved emotions about the relationship, and you've also experienced a tremendous hurt to the self. As a result, boosting your self-esteem—helping yourself become whole again—is a crucial stage of recovery.

The following exercise will help you assess your situation as you start to focus on the self. It's a way of determining how thoroughly you're devoting your energies to meeting your own needs. Take a few minutes to answer this brief questionnaire. For each question, note whether your response is appropriate most of the time, some of the time, or none of the time.

	Most of the time	Some of the time	None of the time
Checklist for Focusing on the Self			
1. Do I consider my own needs and difficulties rather than focusing only on someone else's needs and difficulties?	☐	☐	☐

	Most of the time	Some of the time	None of the time
2. Do I concentrate on living my own life rather than worrying or obsessing about someone else?	☐	☐	☐
3. Do I determine my own schedule rather than waiting for someone else to determine how I should schedule my weekdays, weekends, or vacations?	☐	☐	☐
4. Am I able to say authentically how I'm really feeling and experiencing another person's behavior?	☐	☐	☐
5. Can I ask for what I need without feeling guilty?	☐	☐	☐
6. Can I say no and set boundaries and limits to people's requests, or am I always giving in to what people ask of me?	☐	☐	☐
7. Do I feel that I deserve being treated with kindness, respect, honesty, and equality?	☐	☐	☐
8. If someone isn't treating me with kindness, respect, honesty, and equality, am I able to disengage from this person's behavior?	☐	☐	☐
9. Am I able to ask for help and feel that I don't need to have all the answers?	☐	☐	☐
10. Am I able to be gentle with myself when I make mistakes, and do I see my mistakes as opportunities for growth rather than as failures?	☐	☐	☐
11. Do I have a sense of humor about my own idiosyncrasies, and do I have the capacity to laugh at myself from time to time?	☐	☐	☐
12. Do I take my own needs as seriously as I attend to others' needs?	☐	☐	☐

	Most of the time	Some of the time	None of the time
13. Am I able to be playful and enjoy pleasurable experiences?	☐	☐	☐
14. When I'm upset, do I comfort myself in constructive, positive, nonhurtful ways?	☐	☐	☐
15. Do I speak gently, kindly, and positively to myself when bad things happen, instead of automatically blaming myself and harassing myself with negative comments?	☐	☐	☐
16. Do I have a positive attitude toward my life, and do I see my life as half full rather than half empty?	☐	☐	☐
17. Am I able to take action and be self-motivated and uninhibited when confronted by a crisis in my life?	☐	☐	☐
18. Am I able to be verbally communicative, set limits, and ask for what I want in a direct, uninhibited way?	☐	☐	☐
19. Do I give as much energy and attention to myself as I do to others?	☐	☐	☐
20. Am I able to live in the moment and focus on present events, rather than thinking about the past or projecting the future?	☐	☐	☐

Now review your answers. No answers are right or wrong, and there's no numerical score for your overall response. What's important here is simply the drift of how you've answered. The more often you've checked "most of the time" in response to the questions, the more likely you're attending to your own needs; the more often you've checked "none of the time," the more likely you're neglecting your needs. The degree of attention or neglect corresponds respectively with high or low self-esteem. A preponderance of middle-range responses or a mix of responses suggests a more ambiguous state of self-esteem.

None of these situations is something that you should regard with alarm; they simply provide an overview of how you're perceiving yourself and a sense of where to devote your attentions while focusing on the self. Your answers will help you pinpoint the areas in which you can make positive changes and increase your self-awareness and self-esteem. Consider reviewing this list several months after you first use it, since the passage of time may provide a sense of perspective on whatever changes you experience. Also, try not to tackle more than one or two areas at a time. Attempting to address too many aspects of your self-esteem at once may complicate rather than simplify your task.

The Problem of Low Self-Esteem

Where does low self-esteem originate? For many people, the source is in childhood. Perhaps their parents rarely told them that they were lovable and loved, they didn't hear that they were intrinsically good, or they never learned that they were entitled to more than the task of attending to others. As a result of what many people failed to hear during childhood, they now feel a deep sense of deprivation. That kind of foundation can leave you feeling as if the only way to get your needs met is to be other-focused. Perhaps attending only to others is how you earned your elders' approval. If so, this focus may become a way of soothing yourself, since attending to others' needs is how you perceive yourself as worthy of other people's (and your own) respect. Unfortunately, this arrangement doesn't fully work. Attending only to others' needs may leave you feeling a diminished sense of self.

Beth, for instance, struggled throughout childhood to win her parents' love and approval. Her mother and father were both outwardly successful—affluent professionals in Los Angeles—but they were self-centered, insecure people who provided scant emotional sustenance to their children. Beth attempted to please them in many ways: by being beautiful, by earning good grades, by cultivating "in-group" friends, by attending to her parents' needs to the detriment of her own. Nothing worked. Beth's parents remained almost entirely self-involved. Now middle aged, she continues to feel haunted by an early perception of herself as inadequate or unworthy. Although her parents died some years ago, Beth continues to respond mostly to others' needs and expectations, once again ignoring what she wants from life. The collapse of her most recent love affair has only intensified her feelings that she doesn't matter much.

Why is self-esteem often low in the aftermath of a significant loss? And why does low self-esteem influence your ability to recover? The following are some of the main reasons.

Feelings of Victimization

When you suffer a loss, you may end up feeling victimized. You may feel that you didn't cause the loss or the pain that results from it. This state of emotion can happen regardless of the initial event. Perhaps someone has rejected you. Perhaps you've lost your job. Perhaps someone in your family has suffered a serious illness. Regardless of the specific situation, you may feel as if you're a victim of circumstances. You didn't *want* this to happen! When you realize what has taken place (whether the event is the end of a relationship, the loss of a job, or something else), you feel a sense of shock and dismay that you've been left in the lurch. For many people, one of the effects of this realization is a diminishment of self-esteem. Being jilted feels humiliating. Getting fired from your job causes embarrassment as well as anxiety. Other losses (including those that you know aren't your fault, such as a loved one's illness) also can create a deep sense of helplessness and frustration.

All of these situations damage your perception of yourself as a competent adult.

Feelings of Deprivation

The stress of loss can damage body, mind, and soul. If you're accustomed to someone's presence in your life, separation from that person may leave you feeling deprived. You miss the delights of his or her company. You miss the pattern of your activities together. You miss the sense of definition that your relationship provided—the perception of how you fit into each other's lives and how you fit together into the world around you. The resulting sense of deprivation takes a toll. The aftermath of a close relationship leaves you not only missing the pleasures you shared but also struggling to define yourself anew. This situation is most obvious when longtime spouses end up alone as a result of separation, divorce, or widowhood, but the experience of deprivation can also be intense in the aftermath of other losses.

One of the reasons that you may feel deprived is that your current loss may evoke old losses, too. That is, what you're experiencing now—for example, the sense of rejection that may accompany a failed love affair—can remind you of other kinds of rejection. The old feelings often date back to childhood. This connection with the past may seem irrelevant, but it's not; on the contrary, old feelings of rejection frequently surpass the more recent feelings but intensely augment them, too.

Consider Sally, a woman whose lover ended their relationship. Sally feels sadness, anger, humiliation, and bewilderment because her partner—the man she loves—has rejected her. But underlying these emotions is another layer. This occasion isn't the first when Sally has felt rejected by a man she loves. In fact, she has struggled with a sense of rejection since childhood, when another man, her father, repeatedly left her feeling that she wasn't good enough. As a result, Sally's feelings of deprivation in the present are in some ways only the surface of what she's feeling. Under the surface is the older, deeper layer of hurt and deprivation. Evoking these old feelings has profoundly damaged Sally's sense of self-esteem.

Feelings of Physical Malaise

In addition to a sense of victimization and deprivation, you may also suffer from various bodily symptoms, including fatigue, headaches, stomach pains, respiratory distress, and so forth. These symptoms aren't inevitable, but neither are they uncommon. They are side effects that many people experience following a loss—side effects that both reflect and augment the stresses typical during the grief process.

These feelings of physical malaise are important for two main reasons.

First, they may indicate health issues that deserve attention in their own right. Many of these symptoms (what physicians and psychologists call *somatic complaints*) may ultimately prove harmless, but it's important for you to know for sure. If you're experiencing health problems, you should reassure yourself by getting a physical exam. Symptoms such as exhaustion, shortness of breath, palpitations, weight gain, weight loss, headaches, stomach pains, and loss of appetite aren't uncommon following a major loss, and they often resolve without medical intervention; however, just knowing that your symptoms don't indicate a major health problem can greatly ease your concerns.

Second, these health issues may have another meaning. Even if physical symptoms don't reveal a primarily physical cause, they may be a way in which your body is telling you something about your mind. This issue is, admittedly, rather sensitive. Some people tend to feel that the mind-body link implies that their physical discomforts are all in the mind. This response doesn't reflect what I'm really saying. Rather, what I'm saying is that the mind and the body are so closely intertwined that a jolt to one often jolts the other. The jolt of loss, which we see chiefly as a jolt to the mind, affects the body as well. Should it surprise you, then, that the effects of losing someone you love should influence both your physical and mental well-being? Of course not.

In response to this situation, I have two recommendations: (1) listen to what your body is saying about your body, and (2) listen to what your body is saying about your mind. Sometimes this twofold effort means healing the body—fatigue, chest pains, headaches, or whatever—in order to help heal the mind as well.

The Interactive Aspects of Low Self-Esteem

To complicate matters, the three aspects of low self-esteem—victimization, deprivation, and physical malaise—interact. They don't exist in isolation; in fact, they often complicate and intensify one another. Here's an example.

George, a quality control manager in a large manufacturing firm, had worked almost twenty-five years for the same company. He prided himself on both his technical expertise and his corporate loyalty. Then, despite his accomplishments, the company fired him. George received exactly one day to clear out his office. The reason given for his dismissal was downsizing. George felt stunned, but he put on a good face about the news, emptied his desk, and left on schedule.

In retrospect, he realized that this event had been inevitable. It was common knowledge throughout the industry that his company had been systematically reducing the size of its staff. George knew that his sudden departure wasn't really a result of anything personal. When he lost his job, though, he felt worthless and scared. For decades, he had defined himself as Mr. Quality Control. He loved his work, people respected him, and he had gained great personal, professional, and financial rewards as a result of what he'd attained. Meanwhile, George was in his fifties and at the pinnacle of his career, so he couldn't just walk into any company and start at the ground floor. Anyone who hired him would have to pay him a top salary. The competition was fierce, too, with lots of younger people wanting the same jobs. George knew that despite his experience, many companies would prefer a younger employee at a lower cost. As a result, George felt like a failure as a professional, as a husband, as a provider, and as a parent. "What's this all about?" he'd ask over and over, trying to make sense of his situation. "You're supposed to work hard and give the company your all. Then they repay you like *this*. What does this say about me?"

George responded to his sudden unemployment by isolating himself. Despite an ongoing job search, he had lots of free time, and he spent much of it in his garage workshop. This wasn't altogether bad, for it allowed him a chance to think through what had happened. However, George withdrew to an extreme degree; he isolated himself from his family, avoided other people, and pulled away more and more deeply into a world of hobbies and fix-it projects. He became deeply uncommunicative. He avoided his wife in many ways, including sexually. He also started to experience headaches, panic attacks, and fatigue. George's previously vibrant outlook on life shifted into a hopeless, helpless attitude. In many ways he felt that the world had ended; he had no options; he couldn't cope. The collapse of George's self-esteem left him trapped in a heap of emotional rubble from which he couldn't escape.

This situation is lamentably common. Whether in response to a corporate pink slip or a lover's good-bye note, many people end up feeling paralyzed by a situation that causes a sudden drop in self-esteem. And it's a major issue for men and women alike.

Many American men have been socialized to avoid feeling pain and, even if they feel it, to avoid expressing what they feel. It makes them feel too vulnerable, too dependent, and too weak if they express frustration and sadness over a loss. They worry that they won't be able to "get it back together" and be strong and manly. As a result, George and other men are inclined to withdraw, avoiding social interaction rather than struggling with whatever changes will lead to solving their problems. Withdrawal isn't entirely bad *at certain points in the process*. Many people can benefit from a period of "nursing their wounds" before reengagement with the world. Sometimes it's good to lie low for a while. On the other hand, a protracted period of withdrawal, especially at the expense of meeting obligations to children, spouses, and themselves, can be destructive.

By contrast, women often have a hard time expressing anger for a different but equally destructive reason—they've been socialized to believe that it's not feminine to be furious and out of control. American culture pressures women to be accommodating, understanding, patient, and accepting rather than expressing "bad" emotions like anger. As a result, it's difficult for many women to express the rage that may be necessary for them to experience before regaining their sense of self-esteem. Here, too, self-blame may enter the picture. As with men, self-blame tempts women, for it gives the illusion of being in a more powerful position than is possible.

The Issue of Ambivalence

Compounding the problem of self-esteem is the issue of ambivalence. By ambivalence I mean the experience of simultaneously feeling two or more emotions, often emotions that are diametrically opposed. For instance, you may feel both let down and relieved by the end of a relationship. The situation may be far more complex than what I'm suggesting here; the range of possibilities is enormous. The truth is, human relationships often include many layers of feeling, yet you may be reluctant to acknowledge the complexity of your emotions toward others (if, indeed, you're aware of this complexity at all). Facing and accepting ambivalence—the depth, the variety, and even the contradictory nature of your feelings—may disturb and alarm you.

This issue of ambivalence can also affect self-esteem. For example, consider what happens following an abusive relationship. If you're dealing with this situation, you know that both the relationship itself and its aftermath can damage your self-esteem. How is it possible, you may wonder, that you tolerated an abusive partner? And what does it mean now that you've ended the relationship?

Perhaps you endured an abusive relationship because you felt (as the saying goes) "better off with a devil you know than a devil you don't." At least the problems you faced were familiar. You may have felt demoralized, but you found some security in knowing where you stood. Many people fall into this state of mind. They feel such low self-esteem that they don't consider themselves entitled to more than whatever they're getting. This situation creates a self-fulfilling prophecy. They are more comfortable with the pain and abuse than with the possibility of something better, like a less abusive partner, down the road. Ambivalence complicates the situation because it may leave you fearful of what the future holds. You may feel an intense push-pull: "What am I giving up?" against "What am I going to get?" In addition, you may feel wistful for the known quantity you've left behind, *even if that known quantity was an abusive partner,* precisely because you don't know what's coming next.

To complicate matters even more, ambivalence can include practical concerns. Marge, for instance, knew that she needed to leave her troubled marriage (for both her own sake and her children's), yet she worried intensely about her finances. She had been an at-home mom for many years. Though trained as a dietician, she had been unemployed long enough to make her feel scared about reentering the job market. Would she be able to make it? Could she support herself and her children? Would her husband continue to maintain the family, or would he disengage from the children, perhaps even taking out his anger toward Marge on the kids? Would he completely abandon the family? Marge also worried that she would never find a relationship with a compatible mate; perhaps she'd be doomed to a life of solitude and loneliness. And so she hesitated to separate herself from a man who had made her life miserable in many ways.

Marge's concerns are valid. She should consider the issue of financial well-being (even survival) as carefully as possible. This problem is even more serious for people who may have no vocational training whatever or who have been out of the job market for a prolonged period. There may be significant economic and financial concerns to think through.

At the same time, it's worth noting that the anxiety that Marge feels and that many other people feel as well isn't solely practical. It doesn't even necessarily originate in the relationship that's now ending or that has recently ended. In fact, ambivalence often wells up from a deeper source: the past. What I've described here—the alarm that accompanies separation from a loved one—may have its origins in an older relationship, perhaps even your first relationships, which are those with your parents. What many people feel on attempting to sever a bond between adults is in fact an evocation of powerful emotions—sadness, fear, and feelings of abandonment—that date from early childhood. As infants, we all experienced deep longing for our mothers and fathers. As children, we felt strong ties as well, including a sense of attachment and a consequent sense of alarm at times of separation. Acknowledging the existence of these old feelings doesn't mean that you submit to them; on the contrary, acknowledging them allows you the opportunity to perceive them for what they are rather than to be helpless before their influence. You can then make choices about how to respond to your feelings and their effects—both emotional and practical—on the decisions you make.

Dealing with This Phase of Loss

Given their powerful effects, how should you deal with low self-esteem and ambivalence? The simplest answer is Focus on the Self. Nurture yourself. Allow yourself to feel what you're feeling, ambivalence and all, before you can move on to the later steps of mending your broken heart. Do whatever you can to make yourself whole again.

Here are some suggestions for how to focus on the self, which will facilitate this stage of recovery.

SUGGESTION #1:
Get in Touch with Your Thoughts and Feelings

Most people feel numb following a major loss. This is normal—a way in which your body and mind protect themselves. To recover from loss, however, you must emerge from this state of numbness. That means experiencing what you think and feel about yourself and others. Undertaking this task—which is, in fact, an ongoing process—is strenuous and sometimes scary work. At the proper time, however, it must be done. (I'll address certain aspects of this process in Step 3, "Dealing with the Shadow Side.")

Here's an example of getting in touch with thoughts and feelings. George (mentioned earlier in this chapter) started to improve when he began to get angry. For a long time, he had felt much more sadness and depression than anger. This state of mind was fine initially, but it accomplished little. Once he started to express his anger during psychotherapy, however, George was heading toward recovery. He began to take a stand. He was coming out of that depressed, terrible state of low self-esteem. He stopped blaming himself and started looking at the realities of this life.

One of the reasons that people blame themselves, by the way, is (perhaps paradoxically) that self-blame grants them a sense of power. If George believed that the cause of his firing was nothing more than money—the company was downsizing, and he was a casualty of the corporate drive for higher profits—he would have to admit to himself that he was powerless. He had no control over corporate policy. He felt more in control by saying, "Well, if I'd worked harder, I'd still be working today," or "If I'd gotten along better with my manager, I wouldn't have been given the ax." Self-blame at least allowed him a sense of being in the driver's seat, which George preferred to a sense of helplessness, though the outward results are the same. Unfortunately, self-blame wasn't effective. It didn't really explain what had happened. Only when George got in touch with his feelings—including rage, anxiety, and "why me?" helplessness—could he confront his situation head on and determine how to proceed with the rest of his life.

The following are several methods for getting in touch with your thoughts and feelings.

Find an Ally

You don't have to go it alone. No matter how well you believe you'll figure out your predicament alone, you'll almost certainly do better if you have an ally to accompany you on your journey. This ally can be a psychotherapist, a counselor, a member of the clergy, or a friend. Whoever it is, though, it's important that this person be someone who will listen nonjudgmentally. If you don't have a nonjudgmental friend, find a therapist or counselor who can serve this purpose. You need someone who won't put you down, try to fix the situation for you, or tell you what to do. You need people who are going to listen, love you unconditionally, and validate your feelings. You should avoid people who are unstable in their own lives or who subscribe to the old saying Misery loves company. Find someone you really trust.

Keep a Journal

You can also write down your feelings and explore them by means of a journal. The only rule in this method is not to censor what you write. Your feelings aren't right or wrong, good or bad. They just *are*. It's important to have an uncensored way of getting those feelings out, and a journal is an excellent means to this end.

How should you proceed? Just get started. The particular kind of journal doesn't matter: whether plain or fancy, the style is irrelevant; it's the goal that matters. And the goal is to write exactly what you're feeling—ideally, on a daily basis. You should be entirely open and honest with yourself. You may have feelings that you find shameful, scary, or embarrassing. If so, that's okay. You aren't hurting anyone by setting these feelings down on paper, and the release of these feelings will help to heal you. Allow yourself to feel what you're feeling. The act of writing itself will help you, since it's a safe, helpful way to vent your frustrations, and in the long run this exercise may help you gain a sense of perspective about your experiences.

Use a Tape Recorder

If you don't feel comfortable with a journal, try recording your thoughts and feelings with a tape recorder. Some people don't like to write; they prefer to speak their mind more directly. That's simply a matter of personal preference. Using a standard tape recorder, you can attain the same goal as you would with a journal, with the added advantage of greater spontaneity and (at least for most people) a greater range of emotion. The important thing here, as with keeping a journal, is to be honest with yourself. Also, make sure that you can maintain your privacy.

Whether by means of a journal or tape recorder, the goal is to get in touch with what you're feeling. Try to tune out all the *shoulds*, as in "I should do this" and "I should feel that." Ask yourself these questions:

▲ What do I *really* feel?

▲ What do I *really* fear?

▲ What do I *really* need?

▲ What do I *really* want?

If you keep saying to yourself, "I should . . . I should . . ." it's a red flag waving. Because when you act only on all the *shoulds,* you're often out of touch with what you really feel and need. If you can be perfectly honest with yourself—whether by means of a therapist or counselor, a trusted friend, a journal, or a tape recorder—then you're more likely to get in touch with what you're really feeling.

Talk into a tape recorder, relating the issues I've touched on above. Then play back the tape and listen to it. Reexperience it. This exercise can lead to an acceptance of the complications involved, an understanding of the complexities of the relationship, and a sense of where you fit into your life's events.

Take a Personal Inventory
Assessing your activities, relationships, moods, and assumptions can allow you an opportunity for honestly appraising your life. Here are some questions (similar to those broached in the exercise at the start of this chapter) that you should ask yourself:

▲ Am I overly involved with other people's lives?

▲ Do I give up my personal power, or do I set appropriate limits and boundaries?

▲ Am I lovingly nonjudgmental, or do I try to manipulate and control others?

▲ Do I tend to be passively dependent, or do I take an active role in living my life?

▲ Do I look at life as a glass that's half full or half empty?

▲ Am I positive in my outlook, or do I approach life from a negative perspective?

▲ Do I deal with my feelings, or do I evade them by means of overeating or abusing drugs or alcohol?

▲ Do I reach out for help, or do I isolate myself when I'm in need?

▲ Do I blame others for what happens to me, or do I take responsibility for my part in the process?

▲ Do I inflict guilt and pain on myself and become overly responsible for the problems in my life (or for others' problems)?

▲ Am I often upset by other people's behavior, or am I able to maintain a sense of detachment?

▲ Am I able to give myself tender loving care and take time for myself, or do I focus entirely on other people?

The key in this inventory is, again, to be perfectly honest. Try not to write what you think your responses *should* be; write what you're actually feeling. Feel free to add whatever might come to mind as well.

Practice Yoga or Meditation

Many people find the practice of yoga or meditation (or both) useful in reducing stress, alleviating emotional burdens, and exploring the self. For thousands of years, practitioners of yoga have used this discipline as a method for easing physical and mental strain; in addition, the more advanced yogic techniques can allow access to the mind's inner reaches. Meditation techniques of various sorts can offer similar benefits—not just relaxation but also insights into the nature of your personality. At this stage of the recovery process, yoga and meditation are wonderful ways of centering yourself.

Similarly, sports and other forms of exercise can help you release pent-up stresses and tune in to yourself. Some people, for instance, find that jogging, swimming, hiking, or bicycling can create a nearly meditative state of mind: by occupying the body with a rhythmic form of exertion, these activities release tension and free the mind from nagging concerns.

SUGGESTION #2:
Observe Your Own Behavior

In addition to getting in touch with your thoughts and feelings, you can start to focus on yourself by observing your own behavior. Such observations can help you gain insights into whether you're ignoring yourself to a damaging degree. By behavior I mean whatever makes up your daily life, including

- ▲ work-related activities
- ▲ play, recreation, or leisure-related activities
- ▲ eating habits
- ▲ sleeping habits
- ▲ exercise or lack of exercise
- ▲ socializing with others or isolating yourself
- ▲ sexual relationships
- ▲ exploring new possibilities or being preoccupied with the past

Reviewing these aspects of your life, ask yourself, Is my life balanced? Sigmund Freud remarked once that the healthy life is one that provides a balance between love and work. You might do well to add a third factor: play. How much of your life is dedicated to love, how much to work, and how much to play? The ideal is to attain (and maintain) a sensible balance. Observing your own activities and how you feel about them helps you assess your overall sense of balance.

One way to size up this situation makes use of the following exercise. First, take a piece of paper and draw a large circle. Write the word *love* at the top of the circle (twelve o'clock), write *work* at the lower right (four o'clock), and write *play* at the lower left (eight o'clock). Inside the circle but adjacent to each word, jot down specific activities that fall into the three categories. Note that you may assess which experiences fall into which categories differently from other people. If you really enjoy your job, for instance, it may fall into the category of play rather than work. For most people, close friendships (not just love relationships) can go under the love category. Remember, this exercise doesn't provide a precise assessment, just a sketch. Are love, work, and play evenly distributed among the circle's three sections? Or does one of the three categories predominate? The point here is simply to determine if one aspect of your life is substantially out of balance from the others. If so, then you can compensate for the imbalance by paying more attention to whichever aspect of your life you're neglecting.

Among the other questions you should ask yourself are these:

▲ Do I take enough time for pleasurable activities with others?

▲ Do I take enough time for pleasurable activities alone?

▲ Do I look after my physical health?

▲ Do I look after my mental health?

▲ Do I feel fulfilled or burdened by my work?

▲ Do I feel nurtured and supported by other people?

If you're still so preoccupied with the past that you're neglecting yourself, you might consider what you can change to help yourself become more self-nurturing. Or you can consider changing your attitude about what you're doing. (That is, you may not be able to change the overall situation, but perhaps you can change your attitude about the problem or diminish the stress you're feeling.) In short, focus more energy on yourself. If you're exhausted, get more rest. If you're not eating well, eat better. If you're drinking too much alcohol or taking illicit drugs, stop. If you need help dealing with these problems, find a support group or treatment program. If you're not socializing enough with friends, get out more often.

SUGGESTION #3:
Observe Your Reactions to Other People

Are your reactions to other people really in the present moment— that is, focusing on others *now*—or are you displacing anger or hurt from the relationship you're grieving? Are you responding to the people around you for who they are, or are you projecting your pent-up frustrations, anger, and longing onto others? Try to observe whether your reactions to others are appropriate or not. In the aftermath of loss, you may be shifting your emotions about past relationships onto present relationships. This shifting of emotions carries a double risk. First, it isn't fair to the people you're involved with now, since they shouldn't be caught in the cross fire between you and someone from your past. Second, it isn't really fair to you, either, since you'll miss opportunities for real, here-and-now relationships.

It's worth noting that although isolation is a common risk during the grief process, overinvolvement with others is common, too. Some people flee their oppressive sense of solitude by leaping headlong into a social frenzy. The solace of human company is genuine; however, you can end up having too much of a good thing. The particular issues I'm referring to include compulsive socializing, compulsive caregiving of others, and compulsive involvement in community activities. None of these activities is intrinsically problematic. For many people, reaching out to others can be beneficial. But note my use of the word *compulsive*. The concern isn't participation in social activities, but feeling *driven* to participate. Feeling driven is a potential problem even if the activities themselves are altruistic, such as volunteering at a hospital. The question you should ask yourself is whether you take part in this activity to the detriment of your overall well-being. If so, you should establish some boundaries. Learning to say no isn't selfish; it's self-love, which is a necessary part of attaining and maintaining your self-worth. It's imperative that you learn to set boundaries and limits.

Overinvolvement in others' lives can be a way of distracting yourself from attending to your own needs. It can become habit-forming, and it drains your energy. Part of unhooking from over-involvement is what I call *letting go*. Letting go is relinquishing your need to rescue people, to be the invariably responsible person, to volunteer when everyone else holds back. I'm not saying that participation in specific activities is wrong. It's good to devote some of your time and energy to other people. However, you should (1) maintain a sense of proportion and (2) choose the right time for involvement. In the aftermath of a major loss, you may not be ready to devote a large measure of your time and energy to others' needs. You should attend primarily to your own recovery.

In addition, there's a related issue of self-worth. Many people become overly involved in other people's lives partly because it validates their sense of worthiness. They thrive on the reinforcement that such involvement provides, and this reinforcement vicariously meets certain unmet childhood needs. By nurturing others, you are indirectly nurturing yourself. This overinvolvement can happen even to professionals within the helping professions; many nurses, social workers, and others say to themselves, "I need to be needed." Such a need isn't problematic if you perceive it and understand its effect on you, taking it into account as you make decisions. However, it's important not to need constant approval from others and to know that you're lovable just as you are.

SUGGESTION #4:
Decide What You Really Want

People have fantasies that overly emphasize the external. They think, "If only I moved into a bigger house . . ."; "If only I had a fancier car . . ."; "If only I could marry someone who made more money . . ."; "If only I had blonde hair . . ."; "If only I had a better job . . ."; and so forth. The possibilities are endless—but usually irrelevant. Changing the external aspects of your life won't solve your problems; happiness, contentment, and peace come from within. It's certainly nice to have money and fancy possessions, but material goods won't make you happy. The truth is, you must deal with yourself regardless of how big your house is and regardless of how expensive your car is. And if you're like many people, you risk becoming addicted to external aspects of your life as a way of keeping your spirits up. Material goods function almost as a drug: they make you feel good for a while, but soon the "fix" wears off and you're even more depressed than before.

As a result, you need to find out why you're anxious, lonely, fearful, or angry. Don't focus on external gratification; find out instead what's upsetting you in the first place. How? There are many means to this end. But whether you undertake this search alone or with help (perhaps with a counselor or psychotherapist), the answer usually comes from examining not just the here and now but also your past.

So get in touch with who you really are from the inside. By having those kinds of insights into what makes you tick, you can develop a sense of what you can truly hope for. You can't really develop those hopes if you're out of touch with who you are. You have to find yourself first. Focus on what you need for your own happiness, peace, and contentment.

SUGGESTION #5:
Stop Blaming Yourself

One of the reasons that you may tend to blame yourself for certain life events is that you want to explain the past. You want to gain control of the situation. This impulse is understandable; many people satisfy a need for control by blaming themselves for whatever happened. Does this seem surprising? In some ways it is, but it makes sense in other respects. If you blame yourself for what happened, then you can feel that you're the solution, too. Try to see the situation more realistically, however. People are complicated. Situations are complicated. There isn't any one person who is totally responsible for anyone else's behavior. People come into your life with histories and experiences that you can't be responsible for. By blaming yourself, you may feel that you can really do something to change the situation or improve it. But the truth is much more complex. What happened in the past was more powerful and complicated than what you could have, should have, or would have chosen on your own.

In response to this situation, try to look at situations, people, and events in a way that honors life's complexity. Don't look at things simplistically. There are many events and personal issues that play large roles in any relationship. You aren't so powerful that you can *cause* someone else's behavior. Yes, you play a part in their behavior, but you're not so powerful that you could have caused it by yourself. Similarly, you can't solve all problems on your own. Stop blaming yourself. Try to reach an understanding of what happened within a relationship. I suggest that you think back on the history of your relationship and try to identify the moments that leap out in your own mind. How have you reacted to events, and how did the other person react? What are the patterns that evolved over time?

One way to get a handle on events within a relationship is to write down the other person's childhood history. Write your own as well. This task shouldn't be a formal exercise, so don't feel that you have to do it with great precision or literary flair. It's just a way of trying to see the patterns and connections. For instance, you might discover that you started a relationship with this person partly because of similar backgrounds. Your respective sets of parents treated you in ways that allowed a sense of a common past. Or you had relationships with family members—siblings, perhaps—who helped you feel comfortable with this adult partner. What led you into this relationship? Once you reach a greater level of understanding, your insights can lead you toward new acceptance. Among other things, you may come to accept that you couldn't possibly have been totally responsible for the other person's behavior, thoughts, reactions, and feelings.

SUGGESTION #6:
Try Changing Your Attitudes Toward Other People

If you can't change other people, what *can* you change? This question is one that many people struggle with. The short answer has two parts: (1) you can change yourself, and (2) you can change your attitudes toward other people. Changing yourself and changing your attitudes toward others are, in fact, often two sides of the same coin. Admittedly, both tasks are often difficult. But here are some ways to foster change of this sort.

Cultivate Detachment

Separate your *needs* from your *wants*. Wanting and needing are two different things. The intensity of your wants may, in fact, thwart your efforts to attain what you desire. Everything is a process. Remind yourself that whatever happens, you'll survive—you're strong and you stand on your own two feet. If the relationship or job you want doesn't work out, you'll still survive. You're an independent person. You aren't at the mercy of other people's whims. You're competent and resourceful within yourself, so you'll survive no matter what.

Size Up Your State of Mind and HALT

HALT is a helpful acronym that some people use during the recovery process to size up their states of mind. Whenever you find yourself in a state of fear, doubt, insecurity, or anxiety, use the word HALT. HALT stands for "am I *H*ungry, *A*ngry, *L*onely, or *T*ired?" If you feel one or more of these physical and emotional states, you need to HALT. You should then respond to the situation before getting yourself in trouble. This response can take the form of feeding yourself, understanding the anger or working it off, finding someone to provide company, or getting some rest. There are many possible responses you can make. What's important is (1) to reach an insight into how your state of mind influences you and (2) to intervene before you cause yourself more problems. The HALT idea may seem simple, but it's an effective way to step back from your own behavior and observe it from a wider perspective.

Don't Push Away Your Feelings

Our society is averse to the expression of human emotions. Rather than pushing your feelings away or pretending they don't exist, though, you should let them emerge. *Feel* them. No matter what you may fear, your feelings won't overwhelm you; you're not going to die from feeling angry, sad, hurt, or confused. On the contrary, if you allow yourself to feel your feelings, you'll almost certainly recover more quickly from your loss. Why? Because you're doing what's necessary at this stage of mending a broken heart, which is to focus on yourself.

Once again, what I'm suggesting is easier said than done. How can you choose to feel so deeply when (as is common at this step of the recovery process) your feelings are often uncomfortable, even painful? The answer is that *there is no shortcut around the discomfort or the pain.* Only by experiencing the discomfort or pain can you work through your feelings, move on, and ultimately reach a more satisfying state of mind that lets you live your life in the present. This task isn't something you can force. It's far more effective to sit still, focus on your feelings, and experience them. Let them come up and out. They will diminish over time.

Stop Trying to Change Other People

It's tempting to think that the solution to your problems lies in changing other people. Perhaps you manipulate others into doing things your way. Perhaps you become overly involved in certain family activities. Perhaps you share your opinions in an aggressive way, though others may not have asked for your help in the first place. These are all common ways in which people try to cope with the tensions and frustrations they feel. Unfortunately, they're usually misguided efforts.

Another common reaction—seemingly at odds with changing others—is trying to change yourself *to meet other people's expectations.* You become the ideal partner, the ideal parent, the ideal friend, or the ideal employee. You overextend yourself. You take on disproportionate blame in hopes of swaying others. You try to please others by bending over backwards to accommodate them. You lend them money. You take care of their needs—shopping, cooking, cleaning, baby-sitting. You go out of your way to compensate or cover up for someone else's inappropriate behavior. You may even try to solve someone's personal problems, either by playing psychotherapist or by making that person's appointments with a therapist. In short, you take on a quasi-parental role in hopes that other people will appreciate you and love you, thereby healing the wounds of the past.

Few of these efforts ever work. In fact, most of them are counterproductive. Far from reforming, changing, or transforming others, all you may accomplish is that you increase the distance and intensify the resentment between yourself and others. You mean to be helpful. The people you're trying to help, however, will probably resent your efforts, often fiercely, and feel that you are either acting like a martyr or stepping beyond the boundaries of appropriate behavior. And you won't have solved your problems at all. Again, the only person you can really change is yourself. And you should change yourself *to suit your own development, not to meet others' expectations.*

Stop Giving Up Your Own Power and Diminishing Your Sense of Self

People with low self-esteem often give up their personal power by diminishing their needs and wants. They're so used to focusing on other people—often to avoid their own thoughts, feelings, and needs—that they don't really know *what* they're feeling. They're numb. So one of the ways that people relinquish their personal power is to abandon themselves in the service of others.

Our culture, religious institutions, and families often tell us that we're on this earth to serve others. That's a good attitude in some respects; service to humanity is one of life's best experiences. Even so, this attitude must exist in a proper balance. You're not here only to serve others. You're here also to be loving and good to yourself. And you're only as good to other people as you are to yourself. There's a famous statement by Rabbi Hillel, a first-century Jewish scholar, who wrote, "If I am not for myself, who is for me?" But he went on to ask, "If I care only for myself, what am I?" There must be a sense of balance. You have to focus both on yourself and on others. If you're focused entirely on others, you relinquish your personal power and diminish your sense of self. You lose touch with what you're really feeling and needing.

Try not to feel that you have more control over situations than you really do. You do, in fact, have control over *some* situations. However, you may be convinced that you have more control over other situations than you do. Observe and analyze your situation to decide what truly lies within your influence and what doesn't. Let go of whatever is beyond your control.

When you let go—when you stop trying to control other people—you may (perhaps paradoxically) find improvement in your relationships as a result of your more realistic attitude. The other person feels less pressure from you. You may also find that you're more empowered because you're actually changing what you can rather than forcing issues beyond your grasp and, as a result, feeling frustrated all the time. Once you stop focusing on other people's problems, you may also have more energy. You'll replenish your system. You'll have time to be alone, to think, to reflect, to observe what's happening, and to reach a sense of inner peace.

SUGGESTION #7:
Change What You Can Change; Leave the Rest Alone

Is it possible that you spend time and energy focusing on other people because it's less painful than facing yourself? It's certainly much harder to look at your own past and how you reenact old dramas in the present. Trying to change other people is a huge distraction, however, and can prompt you to lose great opportunities in your own life.

"The past is history," writes Deepak Chopra in his book *The Seven Spiritual Laws of Success.* "The future is a mystery. And this moment is a gift. That's why this moment is called the present." The present is a gift, and we can change the here and now if we live in the moment. Many of us tend to live in the past, or else we fearfully project into the future. It's very difficult to live in the moment. Even so, it's so important to let go and stop ruminating about the future. Ninety percent of what we worry about never comes to pass anyway. But if you're living in the moment, the future will take care of itself. Focus on the *process* rather than the *outcome.* Sometimes what happens is different from what you've expected, but it's often better than what you could have imagined if you kept on pushing and resisting the flow of life.

Let's say that you plant some seeds in the garden. You'll give them water and weed the garden, but you won't constantly dig up the soil to see if the seeds are growing. Similarly, it's fine to have goals in life and to do whatever you can to cultivate them. Go ahead and have ideas about how you want your relationship, career, or family ties to grow, and do your part to bring your goals to fruition. But don't try *too* hard. Don't be so intrusive that you dig up the seeds. Don't work on the relationship so hard that you obsess about it and try to figure out how to manipulate people or situations. Do what you can do, and leave the rest up to nature, destiny, or God. There's only so much you can control.

SUGGESTION #8:
Tune in to Yourself by Following the Three Gs

One way to facilitate your effort to focus on the self is by following what I call the Three Gs—a device for keeping the basic tasks of recovery in mind at this stage.

Guard yourself and pull away from the source of your pain. Separate physically or emotionally (or both) from the person you have experienced as constraining, demeaning, rejecting, or abusive.

Guarding yourself means different things in different situations. If you're disengaging from an abusive partner, take care to guard yourself physically as well as emotionally. This task can be challenging even in the most basic sense of getting away without bodily harm. You may be frightened, perhaps with good reason. Some abusive partners are overtly dangerous; others are more subtle, using psychological pressure instead of physical menace. Either way, however, you may find it difficult to disengage. In such situations, you should obtain counseling and supportive help of any other sort (such as from family and friends). Don't isolate yourself. Make sure that people know what you're up against. You may need to obtain a restraining order against the abusive partner. Contact a lawyer. If you feel you're in immediate danger, find refuge at a transition house for battered partners.

In less drastic situations, such as those involving a relatively nonacrimonious divorce, a sibling feud, or some other conflicted relationship, you can guard yourself in other ways. By this I mean psychologically rather than physically guarding yourself. To the degree possible, avoid putting yourself into situations where the other person will be present. If you have no alternative but to cross paths, such as when there's a family event like a wedding or a funeral, keep your distance. It's likely that you'll bump into the person you're trying to avoid, but you can deal with that if you're prepared. Acknowledge the other person's presence pleasantly, though in a distant way. Stay away from settings in which you'll be harassed or abused. If you are confronted by the person you're avoiding, and if he or she starts to harass you, give yourself permission to leave. "Leaving" may mean simply leaving a specific room. On the other hand, you may have to remove yourself from the whole setting—the church, synagogue, restaurant, or whatever—altogether. The goal is to maintain your separateness as much as possible.

Another aspect of guarding yourself is to avoid revisiting places that intensify your pain. Such places may be old vacation spots, restaurants where you used to meet the person you're now avoiding, or any other site that brings back uncomfortable memories. Create new vacation spots, new rituals, new traditions. Find new people to accompany you during leisure time, and find new places to visit even when you're alone. Don't be tempted by the nostalgia trip—the temptation to steep in memories evoked by old settings and rituals. Build a new life.

If possible, take your time. You may not be able to do so if you're trying to separate from an abusive partner; in other situations, try to let this process unfold at its own rate. For some people, revisiting old haunts allows them to sort through and resolve their feelings. It's not always possible to sever strong ties so quickly. Disengaging emotionally is a process that often moves two steps forward, one step back. Don't be too hard on yourself if you find that you *are* revisiting evocative places. When enough is enough—when you realize that some of the pain you're experiencing is self-inflicted—you'll know it's time to quit.

Gain control throughout the course of your recovery. Take action rather than simply reacting to events that others may create.

Gaining control means knowing your own mind—knowing what kinds of things you like to do, what kinds of tastes you have, what kinds of friends you want, what sorts of qualities you possess, and how you expect to be treated in relationships. By knowing your own mind, you can be decisive, taking action in ways that feel comfortable. Gaining control means setting limits to others' needs, wants, and desires. Don't give up your power by going along with someone else's agenda.

Another aspect of gaining control is knowing your own center. As we've discussed earlier, you can't really change anyone but yourself. Given this reality, gaining control means finding out what really matters to you and then taking responsibility for seeking what you want. Detach yourself from others sufficiently so that you're not enmeshed and simply living someone else's life. Determine the changes you need to make, and then set to work.

Choose a new **goal** that deserves your commitment, whether this means committing yourself to a job, an educational program, a relationship, a hobby, or something else.

The end of a relationship may leave you feeling that your options are closed. On the contrary, you now have many new options ahead. If you're open to all possibilities—if you don't have a rigid idea of what you should be doing—then your new path will emerge. This new goal may mean a development in your education, your career, or your relationships with others. It may mean something less specific, such as changing how you perceive yourself. What's important is that by disengaging from old perceptions and habits, you're now open to new experiences and new ways of dealing with the world.

When you're mending a broken heart, it's crucial to give yourself sufficient time. It's tempting to go berserk, to get involved in everything at once, or to scramble for something or someone to fill the void. Instead, you should tolerate your sense of emptiness for a while. Feel the feelings. Don't push them away. Don't repress them or replace one compulsive relationship with another. Allow yourself time to understand what your past relationships have meant. Give yourself time to reach insights into yourself and others. Otherwise you'll just repeat old patterns over and over. Lie low for a while; try not to fill the void with people, places, or things. If you can stay centered and calm, you're much more likely to perceive what you need to be doing next.

The specific time span for changes of this sort varies from one person to another, so I can't specify a single duration that's likely for everyone. The time will be short or long depending on how much independence you've had in the past, how well you know yourself, and how much therapy you've had before the crisis. If you know yourself pretty well and have been independent, the time span may be shorter than otherwise. What's most important is that you listen to your own sense of timing.

When you feel ready, try experimenting with new activities, ideas, and relationships. Take some risks. Get out and do some things that might have been scary in the past. Take a trip. Sign up for an adult education course at the local college. Join a social group—a hiking club, a gardening club, or a dance class. Pursue a hobby that interests you or one you've never tried before. It's not the specific activities that matter most. What's important is to open up to the possibilities inherent in life and to the opportunities that come your way.

What to Remember About Step 2: Focusing on the Self

▲ Focusing on the self is an important means of boosting low self-esteem.
▲ To focus on the self do the following:
  △ Get in touch with your thoughts and feelings.
  △ Observe your own behavior toward yourself.
  △ Observe your own behavior in relation to other people.
  △ Decide what you really want from life.
▲ Stop blaming yourself for events or situations that lie beyond your control.
▲ Rather than trying to change other people, change your own attitudes toward them.
▲ Tune in to yourself by following the Three **G**s:
  △ **Guard** yourself and pull away from the source of your pain.
  △ **Gain control** throughout the course of your recovery.
  △ Choose a new **goal** that deserves your commitment.

STEP 3

$\mathcal{D}$ealing with the Shadow Side

$\mathbf{P}$atients often ask me why they make choices that aren't in their own best interests or even do things that are clearly harmful to them. A woman who compulsively overeats asks me why she can't control her binges. A man who gets involved with impatient, hypercritical women wants to know why he chooses such unsupportive partners. A woman can't understand why she accepts her husband's emotional abuse. A man feels despondent about tolerating his father's harsh criticism. People want help in understanding what motivates their compulsions, weaknesses, and damaging activities.

Why do we all sometimes act self-destructively? In my opinion, insight can lead to understanding of why we may engage in these patterns of behavior. In many cases, the explanation is what I call the *Shadow Side.*

Our culture (especially popular culture) tends to associate the terms *dark side, shadow,* or *shadow side* with evil. Any number of books, movies, and other media use these terms or refer to them each year. The implications are almost always negative. The Shadow Side is repulsive, harmful, destructive, wicked. It's material for a *Twilight Zone* episode or a Stephen King novel. A deeper and fuller use of this term, however, suggests something much different and much more complex. In fact, this deeper, fuller concept of the Shadow Side suggests an aspect of human personality that makes us the rich, complicated human beings that we are. And the more we get in touch with the Shadow Side—the more we become aware of it, understand it, and work with it in nondestructive ways—the more whole, vibrant, and human we become.

The Nature of the Shadow Side

Sigmund Freud didn't use the terms *dark side* or *shadow side* as such. Nonetheless, his writings show a deep awareness of the human psyche's potential for contradiction and, in some situations, self-damage. There are forces within the personality, Freud noted, that direct aggressive impulses inward instead of outward. Among other things, these drives serve as a defense to protect the psyche from reexperiencing early childhood trauma, such as feeling insufficient parental love. In this sense, the longings and disappointments that people experience during childhood can lead in adult life to self-defeating patterns of behavior.

Carl Gustav Jung devised a more elaborate concept of the Shadow Side—what he called simply the *Shadow*. Jung wrote, "The Shadow consists of the animal instincts which man inherited in his evolution from lower forms of life. Consequently, the Shadow . . . typifies the animal side of man's nature." The Shadow, with its vital and passionate animal instincts, gives three-dimensional form to the human personality.

Though often associated with evil, these impulses are, in fact, quite human. As such, one of the major mistakes we can make is trying to repress them. It's true that we must be socialized; we can't be unsocialized, aggressive beings without jeopardizing our humanity and our society. At the same time, we can't eliminate the animal, primal side from ourselves without significant risks.

Here's an example. Ellen and Alyse are sisters. From birth onward, Ellen was more beautiful than Alyse. Ellen was also livelier, brighter, and more sociable at every stage of childhood. Alyse always felt inferior to Ellen, as well as less loved by their parents. From adolescence on, Alyse sought revenge by stealing her sister's friends and, during their late teens, her boyfriends as well. Alyse didn't even necessarily like the men that Ellen chose as partners; she simply wanted to wreck the relationships. Ongoing jealousy and anger during adulthood prompted Alyse to stage sexual raids on Ellen's love affairs: Alyse seduced her sister's lovers with appalling frequency. Once she concluded each act of sabotage, however, she discarded the men at once. Underlying her behavior was intense self-hatred and low self-esteem. Alyse knew on some level that her actions were both destructive and self-destructive, but she didn't understand the dynamic at work, and she felt helpless to stop acting in ways that sabotaged not just Ellen's love affairs but also the sisters' own sibling bond.

The Pros and Cons of Facing the Shadow Side

Even if you don't believe that your Shadow Side exists, it's still present. It's simply hidden. You may not be able to accept it, but the Shadow Side influences you anyway. Under these circumstances, however, you have no influence over *it*. Until you acknowledge it, the Shadow Side remains a deep, dark, dirty secret. It can feel degrading and frightening. If you already have low self-esteem, you may resist admitting that you have impulses or feelings that seem so dangerous and unpleasant. It's an ego-wounding experience. However, acknowledging the Shadow Side makes it real, accessible, and more consistently subject to your conscious influence. Simply recognizing the Shadow Side is a huge step—more than half the battle. At least now you realize that you don't have to be perfect; you can allow yourself to be human, a person who has multiple dimensions, not just the "nice" sides that are acceptable to society. The Shadow Side is part of you—part of what makes you whole and rich.

Some people wonder if they can move forward, psychologically speaking, if they don't acknowledge the Shadow Side and come to terms with it. In fact, you *can* move on without acknowledging the Shadow Side. Many people do. The problem is that if you don't learn to accept and understand the Shadow Side, you may end up living with less awareness of what's happening, for the Shadow Side will continue to influence you without your grasping how or why.

Jim, whose first love affair provided one of the stories in Part II, is an example of how the Shadow Side can influence behavior. Following his breakup with Sandy, Jim experienced a predictable sense of loss but soon moved on with his life. He felt confident that he would develop other relationships, and he did. What soon troubled him, however, was a pattern that Jim observed in his subsequent love affairs. He seemed drawn to emotionally troubled women. Although he told himself that his frustrating experience with Sandy had been a fluke—just bad luck to fall in love with such an ambivalent, unhappy person—Jim found himself in a series of relationships that bore a striking resemblance to the first. Many of the women he chose as partners were restless, manipulative, and even emotionally cruel. Some of them had significant psychological problems. At times Jim felt as if he were a therapist rather than a friend and lover.

Even when he admitted to himself that the pattern wasn't a coincidence, Jim was helpless to avoid repeating it. Something in his own personality seemed to be influencing him. Later in this chapter, I'll describe what Jim discovered about his Shadow Side.

Many of us are out of touch with all sides of our personality, particularly with the darker impulses or feelings. Under these circumstances, the Shadow Side's influence gets played out in insidious ways including low self-esteem, inhibitions, aggressiveness, inability to be decisive, crises in confidence, inability to take action, inability to feel lovable, and so forth. If you can acknowledge the Shadow Side and accept all aspects of yourself (including the aspects that may not be superficially pleasing or pretty), you may end up having more control over the decisions you make. Denying your Shadow Side may create havoc with your sense of yourself, creating anxiety and depression. You aren't really in touch with who you are and how you really feel. When you understand your Shadow Side, your outside persona—the image of yourself that you present to the world—will be more fully in sync with the emotions you feel within. Under these circumstances, you may attain a sense of serenity and peace that's a real turning point for you. You become more fully in touch with your true nature as a human being.

Methods for Dealing with the Shadow Side

Here are some specific practical methods to consider for dealing with the Shadow Side. Some of these methods resemble those already discussed in this book; however, I've adapted them here to this particular task.

Psychotherapy

As noted earlier in this book, most people can benefit from having a guide to help them explore their psychological workings. The benefits are especially crucial when you explore the Shadow Side. A trained psychotherapist or counselor can ask you appropriate questions or help you see patterns that clarify your behavior now and in the past. While experiencing your life, you may find it difficult to make those connections precisely because the task is so emotional; it's hard to be objective and see the puzzle in its sheer complexity. A skilled therapist can help facilitate insights both into your past experiences and your present behavior. In addition, a therapist can reassure you about difficult aspects of the task as they occur.

Psychotherapy can provide a second chance at being parented again by someone who is consistent, nonthreatening, and perhaps more understanding than your own parents. Obviously, individual practitioners' skills vary; however, a good psychotherapist can provide you with the chance to perceive your life anew. If you tend to form dependent or symbiotic relationships, psychotherapy can help you transfer that need to a consistent, kind love object—the therapist—who in turn can ultimately provide a different vision of intimacy with another person, one that differs from what you experienced in your own family. By this means, therapy can help set the stage for your finding a more nurturing, more loving, less anxious relationship in the future.

Doreen, for instance, felt troubled by her pattern of involvement with older men. A few of her love affairs worked out well, but many were acutely painful. Her experiences with men her own age had generally proved happier; even so, she usually selected much older lovers. Doreen suspected that her past influenced her choices. She even assumed that her relationship with her father played a role. Rejecting this issue as trite, however, she avoided facing it. Only when Doreen explored the situation in psychotherapy did she understand this aspect of her Shadow Side—specifically, a long-standing need to win her father's love and approval—did she loosen its influence on her life.

Keeping a Journal

You can also explore your Shadow Side by keeping a journal of thoughts, feelings, memories, and experiences. As in other applications of this method, don't censor the material. Write by free association, noting whatever thoughts or feelings you experience. Try not to inhibit what you think or feel. Write as honestly and as clearly as possible, without feeling that you have to hide anything or that your emotions are embarrassing or shameful. Note any thoughts or feelings of rage, anger, desires, or destructive impulses. *Anything that you feel you* don't *want to write is probably something that needs to go in your journal.* Don't censor any of those primal feelings, particularly the ones that may make you uncomfortable.

Keeping this kind of uncensored, candid, uninhibited journal is a way of releasing your most intimate emotions in a nonthreatening, safe, nondestructive way. If you're worried about someone finding your journal, make provisions in advance to maintain your privacy. Buy a journal with a lock and key. Better yet, put the journal in a place where no one else can find it. Lock it in your car trunk, in a safe, or anywhere else that's inaccessible to others. The main thing is to find a place safe enough that you don't have to worry. Once you've written your entries, you may end up having a cathartic experience that crystallizes your insights; later, you may decide that you want to destroy or discard the journal. That's fine, too. You don't have to consider the journal a permanent fixture in your life. Think of it as a *process,* not a *product.*

Some people question what this exercise can accomplish. The truth is, you may find that noncensored journal keeping allows a tremendous release of tension and anxiety. It can take a great load off your shoulders. It can even give you a second chance at experiencing life. The reason for this is that you may be able to see yourself differently when you're unburdened by tensions, confusions, and assumptions. Keeping a journal may help you delve back into your past. When you're free-associating, your thoughts, mind, and heart can take you wherever you'll let them go. They may take you back to your childhood. They may project the fears and anxieties you feel about the future. Whatever you feel, whatever comes up, just let it come forth.

Using a Tape Recorder

Using a tape recorder can be useful, too. I recommend this method to people who feel comfortable with it. It can be an easy way of talking about thoughts, feelings, and memories. Sometimes it's less time-consuming than the alternatives. Some of us feel more comfortable with oral rather than written expression. Tape recorders are also interesting because you'll hear in your tone of voice (as reflected in an audio tape) the presence of fear, longing, or anxiety. Certain situations may reflect a younger stage of your development. Perhaps you sound childish. Perhaps you sound angry or confused. Tone of voice can reveal much about your state of mind. One way or the other, the experience can provide a window into what you're experiencing when you record your thoughts and feelings.

Similarly, you may want to experiment with a camcorder. "Interview" yourself on camera, then play back the tape to provide a visual image in addition to the voice. You can see how comfortable or uncomfortable you are with your body or with discussing certain aspects of your life. These experiences can help you develop better self-esteem throughout the recovery process.

Karen Larsson, the woman described in Part II whose parents rejected her for marrying a Jew, experimented with both journals and tape recorders. Baffled by the collapse of her relationship with her entire family, Karen harmlessly vented her sadness, confusion, and anger on paper and on tape. The journal allowed her to record events, to ponder them, and to review a chronology of events that clarified what had happened and when. The tape recorder provided a way of bluntly stating how she felt about these events. (Sometimes Karen literally screamed her anguish and rage into the microphone.) This venting of emotion was worthwhile in its own right; in addition, it revealed certain dimensions of Karen's Shadow Side, including the mischievous, almost wild energy underlying her artistic impulses— an energy that her conservative family found threatening.

Dream Work

Another powerful aid to exploring the Shadow Side is keeping a log or journal of your dreams. Dreams are, in fact, one of the best windows into this aspect of your personality. This journal should be separate from the cathartic free-association journal already discussed.

Here's how it works. Keep a notebook by your bed. Jot down your dreams when you wake. Later, when your schedule allows, compare and contrast what you read in your dream journal with what happens that day or what happened the day before. What do your dreams indicate about your unconscious mind? How do the dreams connect with events during the day? Your goal isn't simply to record and collect your dreams but to understand them within the context of your whole life.

You have several options for how to proceed. Option one is to attempt to understand your dreams unassisted. This is a difficult path to pursue; although feasible, it's not one I recommend, since dreams are often confusing and sometimes upsetting. Option two is to take your dream journal to a psychotherapist to explore together, reaching insights into what your unconscious mind is working through. As is true when pursuing other kinds of psychological insight, having a guide will generally serve you well. Objective perceptions of your dreams may lead to insights you'd otherwise miss. Option three is exploring your dreams in the context of a dream workshop. I advise careful assessment of this option. Although some people who organize dream workshops are insightful and sensitive, others are poorly trained and sensationalistic. Consider reading Jeremy Taylor's *Dream Work,* Montague Ullman and Nan Zimmerman's *Working with Dreams,* or other thoughtful books about dream analysis. (See Appendix B, "Further Reading," for specific citations.)

Letters

You can also write letters—either letters you'll send or letters you have no intention of sending—as a means of releasing thoughts and feelings from the Shadow Side.

Writing but not sending these letters is, ironically, often especially useful. The object is to write to a specific person (perhaps the one you're having difficulties with) and to say whatever you may have left unsaid. This exercise is another opportunity for catharsis. It's a way of releasing anger, expressing disappointment, and airing confusion. Here again, write in an uncensored way, without the other person's feedback to inhibit your feelings and thoughts. The anxiety and fear you've experienced can now surge outward rather than remain submerged. It's a way of getting pent-up feelings off your chest.

I must mention some caveats, however.

First, as with journals, you need to ensure your privacy. Keep these letters to yourself. Hide them in a place that nobody else knows about.

Second, be careful about the urge to send what you've written—especially when the intended recipient is the person you're writing about! *I do not recommend sending a totally uncensored letter.* Writing by free association may be a productive experience, but sending this sort of letter will almost certainly complicate issues between you and the recipient. On the other hand, revising portions of the initial letter may ultimately create a document that you feel comfortable sending. *Consider this option only with great care.* For most people, simply writing the letter and not sending it will be sufficient. Later, you may be glad you never sent what you wrote. Either way, however, this exercise is primarily part of the healing process—a means of expressing and exploring what you feel—rather than a means of communicating with other people.

Letters of this sort aren't necessarily directed to a lover or family member. They could be letters to a former boss, for instance, who you feel has thwarted your career. Again, you won't necessarily send such a letter, for it burns any remaining bridges between you and your past employer and jeopardizes your chances for favorable recommendations in the future. However, writing a letter—even a harsh, angry letter—can allow you to purge yourself of lingering frustrations and resentments. You don't have to suffer in silence. You can speak your mind but in an appropriate way that won't do more damage to yourself and others.

For example, here's a letter that Jan, a registered nurse, wrote but never sent to the head nurse whose negative performance review of Jan led eventually to Jan's resignation.

Pat:

I know you're busy pushing papers, far be it from you to actually set foot in the patients' rooms and see what it's like in the war zone you call your ward, but I want to tell you a thing or two anyway—not that you really care. But I'm doing it anyway, just to tell it like it is. I'm sure you'd ignore this anyway like you've always done, though of course you'd toss off the usual buzzwords about "letting the staff ventilate," as if we're all a bunch of air-conditioning ducts.

One, you may say I'm guilty of substandard performance, but that's 'cause you're more interested in nurses filling out forms than looking after patients. Ask the patients *what they think of me! I bet they'd tell you a thing or two about my performance!*

Two, you said I didn't attend enough in-services. Right (duh!)—because I was so wiped out from working double shifts (and even a few triples) that I couldn't pry myself out of bed during days off to go to workshops. So, yeah, I'm guilty as charged—but not without cause.

Three, you said I wasn't a team player. What the hell *does* that *mean?* I've always busted my butt on duty. I've helped out the other nurses, aides, docs, and everyone else. Lord knows I've done everything I could for the patients. So what team are you talking about? Maybe the softball team when we have our annual picnic . . . ? I can't figure out what you're talking about. Give me a hint.

Four, you said my attire wasn't professional. That's a lot of b.s. The only grounds you have for that accusation is that I used to wear my hair long, but I put it up once DGH changed the dress code. So give me a break. Meanwhile, regarding *your hair, did you know that parting it down the middle makes you look like a water buffalo?!*

No one would mistake Jan's letter for a model of polite correspondence. If mailed, her comments would have severely aggravated

Jan's ex-boss, Pat, and might possibly have inspired Pat to acts of bureaucratic retribution. The letter served good purpose, however, in several ways. It helped Jan enumerate accusations that she regarded as unjust. It let her think through those accusations and consider why they were unreasonable. Perhaps most importantly, the letter allowed her to release her considerable anger in a way that didn't harm Pat but didn't stay bottled up inside Jan, either, in potentially harmful ways.

Speaking with Friends

There's an age-old alternative to those we've discussed so far. "I get by with a little help from my friends," as the old Beatles song has it, and this admission is true for almost everyone. When dealing with the aftermath of loss, however, how much help is appropriate? This question is difficult to answer. On the one hand, we all rely on friends for reassurance, insight, and emotional sustenance. This reliance is appropriate in many ways. On the other hand, it's risky to rely *too* much on your friends. It's not that they're unwilling or unable to help; the problem is that, being friends, they may not be the ideal choice for the support you need. Friends may lack perspective to help you through a difficult time. They may be emotionally close to the person you were involved with, they may remain employed by the boss who fired you, they may have their own emotional agendas, or they may not be able to deal with the intensity of your emotions. So I suggest that you tread carefully when expecting friends to see you through a difficult time.

I suggest that you speak only with friends who are

▲ supportive
▲ psychologically secure
▲ unconditionally loving
▲ empathetic and supportive
▲ capable of listening attentively
▲ unlikely to impose their own feelings and issues on you

Speaking with friends (especially if the friends aren't insightful about themselves and others) all too often exacerbates both sides' anxiety. I repeat, *be selective about the people you talk to.* The kinder, more empathetic, and more unconditionally loving your friends are, the better your chances of benefiting from the conversation. Friends with high self-esteem will be able to listen empathetically without stirring you up or projecting their own emotional issues onto you. They'll listen to you clearly without confusing their issues with yours. Very few people can maintain this sort of detachment. In short, there shouldn't be a lot of people you'll speak with about your loss. If you can't find someone who seems reliable, I recommend finding a psychotherapist instead.

Support Groups

Many support groups exist for people who are grieving, whether in the aftermath of death, or divorce, or some other loss. (See Appendix A, "Information and Support Groups.") You can also look in the newspaper for listings of groups, seminars, and workshops. Likely sponsors are Parents Without Partners, Jewish Children and Family Services, United Way, and Catholic Charities. If there's nothing available in your town, call some of these agencies. They may be able to direct you to appropriate resources. Your local Department of Mental Health may also suggest good support groups; some HMOs do as well.

Should you consider joining a support group? That's a question only you can answer. Many people shy away from this option; they feel uneasy about talking in a group or "airing their dirty laundry" in public. Obviously, this issue is one that you need to examine thoughtfully. In general, however, most support groups are non-threatening; you don't have to take part if you're uncomfortable. Participation isn't mandatory. Also, you remain anonymous in most support groups. At Alanon and Alcoholics Anonymous meetings, for instance, participants identify themselves only by their first names, and one of the stated rules is that "what's said here stays here." Most twelve-step programs start off the program indicating that anonymity is the basis for trust.

Support groups offer the advantage of helping you feel less isolated. You see that others have problems similar to your own. Support groups help you feel that you're not totally alone with your problem and that other people share at least some of your circumstances. Likewise, if you're "stuck" at a particular stage of recovery, a support group can help you to reach beyond yourself to support another person, thus moving you into another stage. It can also help you to feel certain emotions that you might have repressed, since understanding another person's feelings can help you understand your own.

Judy (the woman mentioned in Part II who struggled with issues relating to her parents' alcoholism) found support groups especially helpful. Though not an alcoholic, she benefited from a group setting as a way of understanding her parents' illness. Alanon, a group specifically intended for the spouses, relatives, and friends of alcoholics, provided the support and insight that Judy needed. In this setting, she felt less isolated, she expressed her fears and frustrations, and she learned better ways of coping with her parents.

Are there drawbacks to support groups? At times there are. Let's say that you're proceeding well in your recovery. Encountering people in a support group may tempt you to become a caretaker and stop focusing on yourself. Depending on your stage of recovery, this may be helpful; at other times, however, it may become counterproductive. You may become overly involved in other people's concerns, which can be problematic. Another potential risk is that you may project your thoughts or feelings onto someone else rather than observing what that person is experiencing. If you're too needy or vulnerable, you can't listen nonjudgmentally. Regardless of these risks, however, support groups' advantages outweigh their drawbacks. Making new friends and expanding your social networks can be a wonderful experience. It's certainly very comforting, too, to know that you don't have to suffer in silence.

Spiritual Pursuits

Exploring your own spiritual path can also be an excellent means for discovering your Shadow Side. Again, I'm not speaking of the Shadow Side in the popular sense, with an emphasis on evil; rather, I mean the full complexity of the human psyche, including the aspects traditionally considered spiritual. Many religious traditions stress that until you face your capacity for confusion, ignorance, and destructive or self-destructive behavior, you can't fully understand your capacity for clarity of mind, understanding, and creativity. The great religions of the world are a storehouse of insights into the Shadow Side. For this reason, spiritual pursuits can be one of the best ways to grasp this aspect of yourself.

Heather struggled for years with a conflict over who she was and who she ought to be. Her parents and friends had always tended to peg her as Heavenly Heather, the perfect young lady who could do no wrong and who didn't even feel any "negative" emotions. Rebelling against this restrictive image during her late teens, Heather sometimes played the role of Hell-Raising Heather, the bad girl who partied constantly, slept around, and did everything she could to dash other people's expectations of her. Heather eventually wearied of both extremes. Why couldn't she be just Heather, someone who was psychologically and emotionally complex, someone who didn't have to live life in response to others' simplistic images? Heather used certain spiritual pursuits, including meditation, to integrate various aspects of herself (among them the Shadow Side) until she felt more in tune with her multiplicity of talents, needs, and contradictions.

Exploring a spiritual path can lead to an understanding, for instance, of where your problems fit into the larger picture. You can start to see more clearly who you are, where you're going, and how you can take control of your life. If you believe in a higher power or force or God, your beliefs can help prompt a realization that there's a bigger universe out there; no matter how significant your problems, the larger picture can make those problems shrink to a more manageable size. If you are skeptical or agnostic about God, you can reach similar insights anyway. Experiencing the natural world or the beauties of art can lead to a better understanding of where you fit into the universe. The method you choose is up to you.

Here are some spiritual paths that many people have found helpful in overcoming a sense of loss and grief:

▲ taking part in church or temple activities

▲ studying yoga or other forms of spiritual discipline

▲ meditating or praying

▲ practicing t'ai chi ch'uan, Sufi dance, or other forms of physical meditation

▲ dancing, singing, playing a musical instrument, painting, or practicing some other art

▲ hiking, swimming, running, or engaging in other sports

▲ devoting time to volunteer activities

Exercises for Dealing with the Shadow Side

If you feel ready to deal with the Shadow Side of your personality and if you've decided to undertake this task alone, there are specific exercises you can use to facilitate the process. Alternatively, you can use these exercises in conjunction with a therapist, counselor, or other guide. What follows is *not* a systematic program for dealing with the Shadow Side, however; it's a means for obtaining an overview of this aspect of the human psyche. If you have misgivings about proceeding by this means, listen to what your inner self is telling you. Dealing with the Shadow Side is a long-term task—a process that often takes years—and you're better off taking your time than rushing headlong into it.

The following exercises are all adaptable to the several methods we've already discussed. That is, you can proceed by means of psychotherapy, journal keeping, tape recording, pursuing your spiritual path, and so forth.

EXERCISE #1:
The Shadow Side of Your Family History

Write a family history—either brief or detailed, depending on the amount of time, energy, and effort you want to expend. This history should be a biography of yourself in the context of your family. Be open to what growing up in your family was really like. Although the bright side of your experience may be stronger than the Shadow Side, consider the aspects of family life that were difficult, frustrating, painful, or hurtful.

Start by asking yourself these questions:

▲ What kind of atmosphere did I perceive in my family—tense, calm, antagonistic, pleasant, dull, or chaotic?

▲ What kind of relationship did my parents have—mutually supportive, vindictive, indifferent?

▲ Did I observe kindness, love, and respect between my parents?

▲ Did my parents have an equal, caring, and nurturing relationship?

▲ Were my parents unconditionally loving?

▲ Were my parents supportive?

▲ Did my parents give me positive feedback, or were they critical, controlling, rigid, punitive, or dictatorial?

▲ Did I feel that I had a part in family decisions, or did my parents decide everything?

▲ Were my thoughts, feelings, ideas, and opinions valued and respected?

▲ What role did I play in my family, and how did that role influence my relationships with other family members?

△ Was I the oldest child, the youngest, or somewhere in between?

△ Was I the achiever?

△ Was I the hero?

△ Was I the caretaker?

△ Was I the scapegoat?

△ Was I the mascot?

△ Was I the family cheerleader?

△ Was I the mediator?

△ Was I the peacekeeper?

△ Was I the healer?

△ Or did I have some other role?

▲ What were my sibling interactions like?

△ Were my siblings supportive?

△ Were my sibling interactions competitive?

△ Were my siblings warm and nurturing?

△ Were my siblings hostile and demeaning?

▲ How high or low was my self-esteem during childhood?

△ Did I feel confident or shy and introverted?

△ Did I like myself or dislike myself?

△ Was I confident or insecure?

Jim used this exercise to gain perspective on his situation. Concerned about his recurrent involvement with often needy and sometimes manipulative women, he grew aware that his past might be affecting his choice of partners. Jim eventually started to explore his family background. Writing a childhood history brought several aspects of his past into relief. Jim was aware that his abusive older brother had played a powerful role during his boyhood. Jim was aware, too, that his parents had been supportive and loving toward Jim in many ways. How could this situation, however, have prompted Jim to create troubled love relationships with women? It didn't make sense.

Gradually, Jim understood the connection. Sibling roles had influenced him tremendously. Faced with a disturbed brother, Jim had acquired a role within his family that combined the duties of a diplomat, a peacekeeper, a healer, and a "good kid" whose creative, nurturing presence counterbalanced his brother's negative behavior. Jim tended to feel responsible for righting all wrongs and healing all wounds. Other elements came into play as well, of course; the sibling factor wasn't the only one. But most of the other elements reinforced Jim's sibling role. As a result, Jim often saw himself as the person who would help, comfort, and heal anyone in need. It's small wonder that he tended to pick love partners who also needed help, comfort, and healing.

EXERCISE #2:
The Shadow Side of Your Current Relationships

After you've taken a family inventory, you should look at your current relationships, particularly those that are most problematic. Answer these questions:

▲ What aspects of this relationship are bothering me?

▲ Do I worry or obsess excessively about this problem in my life or this person in my life?

▲ Does this person or situation remind me of someone in my own family or a situation that I saw in my own family when I was growing up?

▲ If so, how does this person or situation remind me of that past person or situation?

▲ When I think about this person and when I reexperience the emotions that I have for this person, what feelings emerge?

▲ Are these feelings reminiscent of those I've had in the past?

Now think about how you would feel if you didn't have this particular person or this particular problem in your life. Answer these questions:

- ▲ How would not having this person or problem in my life change my life, and how would that feel for me?
- ▲ What feelings emerge when I say to myself, "I'm going to let go; I'm going to detach from this person/ problem"?
- ▲ Do I feel physical sensations when I think of this person or situation—longing, "butterflies," headaches, palpitations, or a gripping sensation in my gut?
- ▲ Do I feel tense, anxious, or agitated in response to this person or problem?
- ▲ What would it mean and how would I feel if I let go of this problem or this person?
- ▲ Have I ever tried to let go of a person or a problem in my life before?
- ▲ Do the emotions I feel when I consider letting go remind me of past feelings and reactions?

Jim used this exercise to reflect on how the Shadow Side affects his current relationships. Although currently less "stuck" in his old pattern than in the past, Jim needs to size up his situation periodically to avoid falling into compulsive behavior. His marriage is happy and creative; even so, other relationships are at risk. His interactions with his brother, for instance, sometimes push Jim into the helper/ healer/comforter role that has been problematic in the past. Jim's work relationships could slide in that direction, too. Taking stock of how he perceives people and his ties to them often helps Jim keep his feelings in perspective.

After you've made those connections or parallels, you can begin to have some insight into what has happened in your past and to what degree the past shapes your habitual roles and relationships. Can you break away from the past and establish new roles? Ask yourself these questions:

▲ What would life be like if I didn't have to worry about this person or problem?
▲ How would I change my roles with other people?
▲ What new roles can I envision for myself?
▲ What do I want to see happen in my life?

EXERCISE #3:
Gaining Further Control of the Shadow Side

Next, write a wish list. What do you truly want? Serenity and peace? Not worrying about what you've lost? Learning to focus on yourself? Now write an objective time line of some steps you can take to accomplish what you wish for. These steps could involve taking a class, getting involved in psychotherapy, finding a support group, avoiding an abusive partner—whatever you feel will help you start the process of letting go and moving on so that you don't keep replaying those aspects of the Shadow Side. Then try to do things differently. A time line can be useful; on the other hand, a list of goals without a time line may be more helpful. Either way, don't be hard on yourself. Be gentle. Choose realistic goals. Keep in mind that we all slip up, and many times we take a step or two backward just before taking a giant step forward.

The Challenge and the Reward

Both as a therapist and as a human being, I feel obliged to state outright that exploring the Shadow Side is a major challenge to most people. It's a journey that is usually difficult, often painful, and potentially scary. I recommend that if possible you undertake this task with some kind of guide, whether a therapist, a counselor, a member of the clergy, or some other kind of spiritual teacher. You can make the journey alone, but you may feel safer and more comfortable with guidance.

Some people ask me why they should explore the Shadow Side at all. Isn't it better just to let sleeping dogs lie? The answer to this question is complex. One of the main reasons for exploring the Shadow Side is that by doing so, you won't have to live in the state of doubt, insecurity, and anxiety characteristic of some people who remain unaware of this aspect of their human nature. The Shadow Side will influence you whether you face it or not. Facing it, however, will leave you more knowledgeable about the nature of its influence, and this knowledge in turn allows you more choice over and protection against previously hidden and potentially self-destructive forces that alter your behavior. Knowledge is why exploring the Shadow Side is worthwhile. Until you're ready to deal with the negative side of your personality, you're relatively helpless to understand its effects on your life. And you're not really living life to the fullest. Coming to terms with the Shadow Side gives you the opportunity to live without being so controlled, controlling, obsessed, driven, and tense.

When someone has broken your heart and left you feeling devastated, the experience shakes your entire world. You feel that you're never going to be whole again. Once you come to terms with the Shadow Side—the side of your personality that may be compelling you to repeat painful experiences from the past—you may experience a profound sense of freedom. You have more energy because you're expending less energy on self-defeating fantasies and efforts. You're stronger internally. You have a self again. You don't have to waste so much energy trying to fix or control the people who are beyond your control. You are much more stable. And then, having accomplished what you have, you'll have a tremendous amount of energy that you can put to better use on more positive activities and goals.

What to Remember About Step 3: Dealing with the Shadow Side

▲ Dealing with the Shadow Side is a necessary step to recovery following loss.

▲ The Shadow Side isn't what popular American culture considers it—evil—but instead is a composite of aggressive, instinctual, and sometimes compulsive tendencies within the human personality.

▲ Ignoring or denying the Shadow Side won't prevent it from influencing you.

▲ Acknowledging, facing, and exploring the Shadow Side are the only ways to gain control over it.

▲ Methods for dealing with the Shadow Side are varied, but those that include assistance from an experienced counselor, therapist, mentor, or other guide are often especially effective.

▲ Carefully consider your readiness to face the Shadow Side, as the task is often challenging; however, the rewards are great.

STEP 4

Stabilizing Your Life

As I mentioned in Step 3, dealing with the Shadow Side is (like every other aspect of mending a broken heart) a process rather than an event. It doesn't happen quickly and certainly not all at once; in fact, it may involve a long-term commitment to gradual change. At some point, however, your efforts will pay off. You'll begin to have a better sense of how past experiences influence your perceptions of yourself. You'll start to understand how unconscious motivations affect your behavior. You'll gain more control over your decisions at work, in your love life, and in your family interactions. These changes will suggest that you're starting to stabilize your life.

It's worth noting, too, that to some degree you'll simply work yourself through the most intense phases of the grief process. I'm not saying that you'll ride the process effortlessly; rather, I mean that your mind, heart, and soul will benefit from their own capacities for growth and regeneration. Time may not heal all wounds, but time is nonetheless a necessary component of both physical and emotional healing. If you trust the process, your patience will serve you well.

I must offer this caveat, however. We live in a culture in which patience is neither valued nor cultivated and where haste is often considered a virtue. Even if you manage to stay patient with the grief process, people around you may not. Well-meaning friends and relatives will be prodding you to "get it over with," and they will at some point wonder out loud why you aren't over him or her yet. They'll say, "Get back into the swing of things!" "Move up and out!" "Don't mope around and brood!" In response to these exclamations you can only say, "Well, yes—at the right time." But give yourself the time you need. Stabilizing your life means slowly—often *very* slowly—returning to a reality-based life. The grieving process takes time. You can't force it to happen any faster than your own heart will allow. If there's a single significant risk that most people face at this time, it's impatience. As a wise person said long ago, "Don't push the river."

The catch, however, is that you must continue all your normal daily activities while grieving; you must work, look after children, carry on relationships, manage finances, do the laundry, cook meals, clean the house, and so forth. These multiple tasks can seem overwhelming when interwoven with the already difficult grieving process. You're experiencing strong emotions, struggling with intense memories, and trying to make sense of your life. At the same time, you're going through the physical motions of everyday living, but your mind and heart are still in a state of shock and numbness. How can you perform both the internal tasks and the external tasks simultaneously?

The truth is, getting back to a reality-based life happens in stages. The process doesn't happen all at once; you begin to feel better little by little. Many Americans believe that a normal, healthy person can get over a loss in a few months—a year at most. For most people, grieving requires a longer interval than that. Some people need less time, but many require more, a year or even several years. To complicate matters, you may go in and out of the grieving process. Despite the popular image of grief as something that occurs in fixed, time-limited stages—shock, numbness, anger, acceptance, and so forth—you may or may not experience the process sequentially. You may experience a period of intense grieving, then a period of relative calm, then another period of grieving, and so forth. And what is normal for someone else isn't necessarily what you will experience.

Tamara, despite having lived with her lover, Jerome, for many years, felt surprised by how quickly she recovered from their breakup three years ago. Should she have felt more upset? She wondered at times why she was so minimally affected by her loss. In fact, she *was* affected—just not as severely as she had expected. The relationship had been satisfying for a long time but gradually became more frustrating and troubled. Eventually it seemed high time to move on. There's nothing wrong with that.

By contrast, Celeste considered herself "demolished" when her longtime lover ended their relationship. She couldn't imagine going on without him. Her life seemed to have ended. Of course it hadn't; she recovered, reestablished her place in the world, and ultimately found new people to love and enjoy. The severity of her grief took her by surprise, however, and required more patience and effort to accept and endure than she had anticipated.

Whatever else, stabilizing your life means realizing that life as you knew it will never be the same. The relationship you had, the person you loved, or the job you enjoyed are now gone. Those relationships, people, and activities organized your life in certain ways. Now that organization has changed. To live a new reality-based life, you must create a new vision based on how your loss has transformed you—how the experience of loss has changed you as a person, as a partner, as a worker, and so on. Only by accepting the loss and its consequences can you reach understanding, insight, and the potential to move on to the rest of your life. And as you stabilize your life, you will once again experience the pleasures of living in ways that may have diminished during the grieving process.

Why Is This Step So Hard?

Like the earlier steps of the grief process, stabilizing your life can be difficult. There are many reasons why it's hard to move on. Here's an overview of the difficulties and how you can respond to them.

The Hard Work of Grieving
The grieving process is often painful, confusing, and strenuous. It's difficult work to feel your feelings, process them, understand them, and gain insight into them. Perhaps this situation seems obvious, but many people are surprised by how hard they have to work during the grief process. Worse yet, grief is *painful*. Obvious again? Maybe so. But the pain, too, takes many people by surprise. "I can't believe how miserable I feel," a friend told me following the end of a long relationship. Well, why not? You've lost someone you cherished. Your life has changed. You're struggling to determine what happens next. It's no wonder you're in pain.

My response is that the painful feelings you experience—the sense of loss and anger, the shock, the disbelief—are all part of the process. They're a necessary phase of working through your loss and stabilizing your life. If you can accept them as part of the process, they're less likely to obstruct you in the long run. If, on the other hand, you build a hard outer shell around yourself to avoid experiencing the pain of the loss, you'll actually delay your recovery.

Idealization
In the aftermath of loss, you may end up idealizing what you've lost. The reason for this is that you had formed an identity through a person, relationship, or job. This situation is understandable. Idealization of this sort, however, may complicate your task of moving on, since you probably attribute a lot of your own positive attributes to what you've lost. Seeing the other person or job in such a favorable

light, however, isn't necessarily a helpful state of mind. You may have built your identity around the other person or situation because your own personality felt incomplete. You weren't whole to begin with. For this reason, you lived through the other person or relationship. This state of mind is part of idealization and, in turn, a source of why you feel reluctant to give up your fantasy. You have idealized what you loved so you can define who you are.

Here's an example of idealization. Natalie is a forty-year-old physician. For many years she felt supremely confident, and her marriage to Mike, a handsome and well-regarded research chemist, had always bolstered her confidence. The couple's relationship was intellectually stimulating and physically passionate. Then, without warning, Mike fell in love with a twenty-year-old aerobics instructor. He moved out of the house he shared with Natalie and demanded a divorce.

Natalie needed years to get over this sudden loss; even once her recovery was well under way, though, she struggled to understand the implications. It wasn't just that Mike had rejected her. He had rejected her for a gym teacher! Natalie couldn't figure out what this meant. Did it mean that she didn't have enough "goods" (whether intellectual, emotional, or sexual) to hold Mike's interest? Did it mean that she had overestimated what Mike had to offer? Did it mean that Mike was as remarkable as she had assumed but had entered a "middle-age crazy" phase? She couldn't decide. But during the process of coming to terms with her loss, Natalie's hardest work focused on understanding the idealized image she had created both for herself and for Mike.

Idealization is a normal part of grieving. This response is especially common when loss has occurred in the aftermath of a death. However, it's also common when the loss has occurred by other means. You shouldn't berate or criticize yourself for idealizing the now-lost person or situation. At the same time, you need to understand what you're doing and what consequences can result from this state of mind.

The Fantasy Bond

In earlier chapters, I've noted that the fantasy bond—the image you have of the other person—often echoes your first intimate relationship, which is the relationship between you and your primary parent. (For most people, this relationship is with the mother.) Whether this relationship is with your mother or someone else, a lack of security in that primary relationship can prompt you to look for what you're missing in other relationships. You may look for a quasi-parental closeness in your romantic relationships, for instance. You may also become much more attached to other people in ways that resemble an infant's attachment to his or her parents. In other words, you may substitute one primary love object for another. Sometimes this means substituting one relationship for another. For example, you may rely on your spouse or lover for a parental kind of affection. Sometimes it means expecting a career to provide the sense of identity you crave. Either way, this fantasy attachment resembles what an infant wishes for—an engulfing sense of love, a sense of oneness with the other person. The truth is, however, that we have only one mother and father, but we don't have only one potential adult love relationship, only one meaningful job, and so forth. Fantasy bonds may burden your adult relationships with excessive, inappropriate expectations.

Repetition Compulsion

Stabilizing your life may also be difficult because the treatment you've experienced in an adult relationship is familiar from childhood. Finding your situation familiar, you may attempt to stay loyal to a damaged relationship as a way of winning an unobtainable love object. You desperately want acceptance and approval because you couldn't find it in your early years. Thus it becomes difficult to let go precisely because you feel a compulsion to get it right this time—to win at last.

An example of this situation, in the story of Jamie, is one described in Part I. Despite Jamie's intelligence and personal accomplishments, she felt a compulsion to relive a conflicted father-daughter relationship by choosing men who, like her dad, tended to be powerful, controlling, and emotionally remote. It's not that she thought she would ever regain her actual father's love; he had died during her college years. Having become accustomed to the manipulative and self-serving behavior of powerful men, however, Jamie found this situation so familiar that she gravitated toward people like her dad. Her unhappy love affairs were, unfortunately, a kind of memorial to the power of her longing for Father. Jamie's most difficult task while stabilizing her life has been to understand her repetition compulsion and its almost invariably disruptive consequences.

This kind of scenario often exacts a huge cost. The reason is that under these circumstances, you may link up with people whose behaviors and personal characteristics, though familiar, mimic those of your neglectful or inattentive parents. Oddly, the neglect makes you feel comfortable. However, this situation doesn't create more stable relationships; on the contrary, it continues a situation notable mostly for its instability.

Economic Insecurities

Some people fear financial hardship in the aftermath of leaving a marriage, dissolving a partnership, or losing a job. Such fears may be realistic. Following a divorce, you may in fact experience a lower standard of living. Likewise, losing a job may create short- or long-term money problems. For these reasons, economic concerns may influence how you perceive the aftermath of loss. These concerns aren't necessarily inappropriate. At the same time, they needn't be the determining factor in your decisions; they are one element of many to take into account.

One partial response to the problem of economic insecurity is to assess your finances as fully as possible. Such an assessment may not solve all the problems you face, but it's a necessary start to knowing at least what the problems are. Having identified the specific issues you face, you'll be in a much better position to decide on the appropriate response. You have several alternatives in making this sort of assessment:

> ▲ If circumstances allow, consult with a lawyer, financial planner, or both.
>
> ▲ If your finances constrain you from this course of action, try to obtain information from other sources, such as books, computer programs, pro bono services, toll-free advisory hot lines, etc.
>
> ▲ Under some conditions, a knowledgeable, professionally trained friend can also be helpful (though you should be careful of potential conflicts of interest).

Appendix A, "Information and Support Groups," includes information about several resources you may find useful in this regard.

A Sense of Failure

When a relationship ends, you may feel that what happened is somehow your fault. You should have done better. You should have forced the situation to continue. Many people feel this way; they believe that what happened isn't just the nature of the circumstances but is in fact a personal mistake.

Why do people blame themselves for situations that are probably far more complex? You may be feeling so beaten or battered that you simply don't feel confident or strong enough to deserve anything better. A more realistic perception, however, is that you took the situation as far as you could but simply couldn't take it further. You worked on your marriage but couldn't save it. You gave the job your best, but other circumstances intervened. You tried to get along with your sibling but couldn't heal the rift single-handedly. You aren't the sole determinant of what happens.

Karen Larsson struggled with a sense of failure for many years. At times she regarded the rift with her parents as totally her fault. She shouldn't have made such an abrupt move from home; she shouldn't have taunted her mom and dad so openly about their provincial ways; she shouldn't have criticized them so bluntly about their intolerance toward her Jewish husband. These were just a few of the accusations that Karen leveled at herself. Karen may indeed have contributed to the rift. There's no reason for her to carry the whole blame, however; her parents deserve a large measure of responsibility for what ensued. Ultimately, blame serves no purpose. Karen certainly does herself a disservice by trying to shoulder the whole burden.

Hesitance to Take Another Risk

Following what you've been through, perhaps you don't feel ready to take another chance again. You're in shock. You don't trust other people now. You no longer even trust your own judgment. Under these circumstances, you may have a difficult time taking chances again—finding the courage to build new relationships after you've felt betrayed by a spouse, a partner, a family member, a boss, or a friend. This state of mind isn't surprising. Many people feel paranoid when their confidence has been deeply shaken. This situation, too, is normal. Here again you may find moving on difficult, since you feel that your efforts are causing you grief. The answer to this dilemma, though, isn't to give up altogether; the answer is to pace yourself, allow yourself to grieve, and then move on when you're ready.

How to Stabilize Your Life

Following are three practical recommendations for stabilizing your life.

RECOMMENDATION #1:
Cope with the Here and Now

You may feel ambivalent about letting go because you feel a push-pull sensation—a sense of attachment or lingering love—despite whatever negative emotions you feel as well. In addition, day-to-day issues may complicate your response. It's often difficult, for instance, to deal with the ordinary tasks of living and somehow detach from your emotions. You can't turn your feelings on and off like a faucet. At the same time, you can't ignore the daily tasks that face you. This cluster of frustrations is notoriously difficult in the aftermath of a divorce, when ex-spouses must still cope with practical issues, such as those concerning custody and childcare. But intense issues can crop up in other situations, too, such as those following the separation of nonmarital partners, the end of a job that involves lingering professional duties, and so forth.

Here's an example. Divorced many years ago, Marla still has frequent contact with David, her ex-husband, since she must interact with him about their daughter, Sandy. Marla and David discuss the child's schedule of activities; they transfer Sandy from one house to another on weekends, holidays, and vacations; and they cross paths at teacher conferences, school plays, or other child-related activities. Other social events in their small city also bring the former spouses into contact. "Seeing David really stirs up pain from the past," Marla admits. "I'm glad we're divorced, and I have a new life now. But it's difficult to let go completely when I'm still confronted by this person several times a week. It's like he keeps rising from the dead. How can I put him to rest when he's showing up all over the place?"

Marla's comments suggest something that I've perceived in many people: divorce, separation, or other interpersonal rifts can create a loss that's as difficult, if not more difficult, than the loss following a death. Loss following a death is permanent. You'll never see that person again. Although wrenching and terrible in many ways, this clear-cut loss at least lets you know where you stand. The relationship is over. With divorce (and with the termination of other love relationships), however, the separation is more ambiguous. You don't sever the bond in such a total way. You have to learn to tolerate a degree of ambiguity. Holidays come and go; anniversaries and birthdays approach and pass. Today was your anniversary, you realize. This gathering is how we spent Christmas last year. That restaurant is where we had Thanksgiving dinner three years ago. Whatever the nature of your past celebrations, the year's cycle of days can rub you raw.

Another complicating factor is when the other person acts in manipulative or hostile ways. Someone you once loved may behave in a manner that's intentionally provocative or cruel. Sometimes this behavior involves petty actions, such as arriving late at scheduled meetings or gossiping about you. At other times the behavior is more severe. Your former spouse withholds child-support payments. Your ex-boss, having promised you a good recommendation, writes a negative reference letter. Your ex-partner sues you for frivolous reasons. Your sibling lies behind your back and manipulates other family members against you. In these and other circumstances, your task isn't just dealing with the loss you've suffered; it's also dealing with how the other person responds to you. The combination of your own and the other person's behavior can complicate the task of letting go.

In such cases, what should you do? It's hard to generalize, but I suggest that if possible, you should do what is good for you and (when relevant) for your child. Evaluate the situation. Get legal or psychological counseling whenever possible to clarify your thinking. At times you can continue contact with your ex, your in-laws, or whoever else was once part of your life. If this feels comfortable, it's fine for you and your child. Under other circumstances, however, you may have to make more clear-cut separations between your old situation and the new. This may mean no contact at all with your former spouse, partner, lover, or family member. You must evaluate the situation on an individual basis. Make the decision and set the boundaries that you find comfortable.

RECOMMENDATION #2:
Cope with the Past

You may tend to transfer a lot of feelings from past experiences to your present relationships with friends, colleagues, and lovers. This tendency isn't uncommon. In fact, it's almost inevitable. *Transference,* as psychotherapists call this phenomenon, is part of being human. The problem occurs when you transfer these emotions *without awareness of what you're doing* and without having resolved any lingering problems from your past. How should you respond to this situation? The short answer is that you should evaluate how much of your relationship with someone in the present is being invaded by ghosts from the past. The long answer is that you need to grasp the influence of past relationships in the present.

For example, Janice grew up in an alcoholic family. Both of her parents were needy, difficult people who relied on their only daughter to define and organize their lives. Janice became the parent in her family; her parents became the children. The stress of this situation prompted Janice to move out of the family home right after high school, because she wanted to get away from her burdensome parent-child relationship as fully as possible. Once grown, however, Janice married Peter, who resembled Janice's parents in his being helpless, disorganized, and abusive. She soon became more of a parent than a wife. Peter remained dependent—unemployed, emotionally desperate, and behaviorally unpredictable. He was critical of Janice and controlling of their relationship. Janice was stronger than Peter; unfortunately, she lacked sufficient self-esteem to set limits with her husband and ask for what she wanted from him. Having grown up in a dysfunctional family, she felt accustomed to the caregiving role, and she never felt entitled to have anything for herself.

Janice gradually loosened the past's grip on her life. Through psychotherapy and her own growing insights, she understood the connection between her pseudoparental role during childhood and her pseudoparental role in her marriage. Understanding the connection didn't magically free Janice from behaving like a parent toward her husband. Her insights allowed her to start taking control of the situation, however. And as she stabilized her life, she managed more and more consistently to define a more appropriate spousal role for herself and, simultaneously, to set limits on her husband's dependent behavior.

In the discussion of earlier steps of the recovery process, I've suggested several methods for dealing with the past and easing its power to control your actions in the future. These methods are just as useful when trying to stabilize your life as when dealing with earlier steps of the process. If necessary, review the possibilities by rereading pages 105 to 109 in Step 2 and pages 129 to 140 in Step 3.

RECOMMENDATION #3:
Change What You Can and Disengage from the Rest

In this step of the recovery process, as in those preceding, part of your task is to determine what you can change and what lies beyond your grasp. The issues are the same as before. The main difference at this stage is that (ideally, at least) you should be further along in your ability to distinguish what's changeable and what isn't. Once again, the focus of your efforts should be yourself—your own attitudes, your own actions, your own present, your own future. And the realm that lies beyond your grasp is, predictably, the people around you.

The following exercises can assist you in this task.

Exercise #1: Cause and Control
This exercise is a way of helping you realize what you can and can't change in life, with emphasis on the "can't" side of things. Take a piece of paper. Draw three columns. In Column 1, list some issues or events that you *can* control. In Column 2, list some things that you *can't* control. In Column 3, write down what you can do about the issues and events in both Column 1 and Column 2.

Let's say that alcohol abuse has been a problem both in your family of origin and in your own adult life. In Column 1, "Things I Can Control," you write, "Stop drinking so much." Beneath that (once again in Column 1) you write "Stop Dad from drinking so much." Then, writing in Column 3, "What I Can Do About It," you write "Contact A.A." in response to your own Column 1 entry and "Make Dad go to A.A." after the entry about your father's drinking. Now look at what you've written and consider the implications. You can, in fact, respond to your own alcohol abuse by contacting A.A. and attending their meetings; this situation is one in which you really do exercise some control. Regarding your dad, however, can you realistically expect to *make* him attend A.A.? No. You can suggest that he contact A.A., and you can tell him that you intend to attend some A.A. meetings yourself. But it's not realistic to think that you can make your father (or anyone) stop drinking or even make him attend A.A. Those actions are ultimately his own responsibility. The words "Stop Dad from drinking so much" realistically belong under Column 2, "Things I Can't Control."

In short, outlining the situations can clarify where you can exert real control and where you can't. And the outlook is generally that you exert control primarily—often exclusively—over yourself. There are exceptions; if you are a parent of minor children, for instance, you have both a responsibility and an ability to influence their behavior. But with adults, your influence is almost certainly focused on your own life and the choices within your grasp.

Exercise #2: The Mirror

The second exercise uses a mirror as a device for prompting you to perceive yourself anew. Of course you look at yourself in mirrors every day, but do you truly *see* yourself? This exercise encourages you to look more closely and then to verbalize to yourself about what you see both physically and emotionally.

Here's what you do. First, find a convenient mirror. Then, with a pad of paper and a pen or pencil nearby, look at yourself. Now answer these questions:

- ▲ What kinds of emotions do I feel when I look at myself?
- ▲ Do I see someone who looks in harmony with himself or herself?
- ▲ Do I see a tense, strained face?
- ▲ Do I look relaxed and rested?
- ▲ Do I look fatigued and haggard?
- ▲ Do I look well-nurtured and provided for, or do I look as if I haven't been taken care of, whether by others or myself?
- ▲ What else do I see that suggests my physical and emotional state?
- ▲ Am I comfortable looking at myself?
- ▲ Does this exercise itself make me uncomfortable?
- ▲ What would I like to change about how I'm feeling?

Take a good, hard look. Then write down what you see on the pad of paper. This exercise is a means of becoming more attuned to yourself physically, emotionally, and spiritually. By writing your responses and reflecting on them later, you're experiencing your feelings rather than focusing on external events or other people.

The Leap of Faith

In Step 2, we noted that loss often lowers your sense of self-esteem and that regaining your self-worth is part of the grief process. Since you may experience a low ebb of self-esteem in the aftermath of a major loss, how can you undertake this step and start rebuilding your life at a time of limited emotional resources?

First of all, you must have an awareness that you are not truly yourself at this particular time. You aren't functioning at full capacity. You've lost part of yourself in the aftermath of loss, and it's going to take time to regain that sense of self and rebuild your life. The grieving process is slow. It takes a long time to rebuild your life, especially when you're rebuilding your life from the inside out. Yes, you can move from one house or apartment to another, you can find a new partner, and you can get a new job. But making internal changes—learning to respect yourself, opening your mind and heart to new possibilities, and giving your wounds and injuries time to heal—is a difficult, long-term task.

Paradoxically, when you let go of the relationship, you will regain your self-esteem; at the same time, you need to have enough self-love to say that you deserve something better than what you've had until now. This situation requires a leap of faith. Sometimes taking a leap of faith occurs when you've actually reached the bottom; your pain exceeds your longing for the past, and you decide that enough's enough. If so, then you can decide that staying in an unhealthy relationship isn't what you want—or even what you'll tolerate. At other times, a leap of faith isn't so severe; it's a gradual withdrawal from the situation or the person, a task of building another life while you simultaneously stay connected to the old relationship or job. Either way, the very act of moving on may be what empowers you to do precisely what you're doing.

Taking a leap of faith doesn't mean an instantaneous, radical transformation. It doesn't mean totally changing your life. What it does mean is opening yourself to possibilities. Taking a leap of faith needn't threaten you; rather, it means cultivating other paths and other choices. Taking a leap of faith can boost your self-esteem and, in turn, give you the sense of mastery you need to stabilize your life.

What to Remember About Step 4: Stabilizing Your Life

▲ No matter how difficult it feels to recover from loss, your efforts will eventually pay off and you'll stabilize your life.

▲ You may find this step of recovery difficult for several reasons:

△ The grief process is inherently hard work.

△ You may tend to idealize whatever it is (the person, relationship, or job) that you've lost.

△ You may cling to old images (left over from childhood) of a fantasy bond that continue to influence your present-day situation.

△ Practical issues (such as financial pressures) may complicate your ability to separate from old situations or relationships.

▲ You can simplify the task of stabilizing your life by

  △ focusing on the here and now

  △ acknowledging the power of the past

  △ changing what you can and disengaging from the rest

▲ Ultimately, you must take a leap of faith to open yourself to new possibilities and give yourself what you really need from life.

STEP 5

*B*ecoming Aware of
Your Recovery

How do you know when you're getting better? Step 5 of the process is something you can't *make* happen; it simply happens on its own. This step is growing aware of your recovery. The most obvious signs that you're on Step 5 are a renewed sense of well-being, new success in the outside world, increased pleasure in your activities, and a greater degree of commitment to other people. Perhaps you've found new friends or have started another love relationship. Perhaps you've landed a new job. In these and other ways, new commitments suggest that you're starting to rebuild your life.

It's important to note, however, that this stage (like those preceding it) varies from person to person. It's normal for the grief process to be a two-step dance between regression and progression. You may feel at times that you're losing ground—taking more steps backward than forward. If so, relax. You can't *make* yourself recover, though you may try to hurry the pace. This temptation is counterproductive because you're forcing premature and often inauthentic solutions on your recovery. Rushing things may backfire and ultimately complicate your life. Give the healing process time. Haste may cause problems in the long run.

Just as you can't force the recovery process itself, you can't force your awareness of recovery. How do you know you're getting better? The truth is, it's sometimes hard to tell. You can, however, tune in to how you're feeling and how you're behaving both alone and with others. The more you tune in to certain little things (which aren't really so little), the more you'll be aware of significant signs of your recovery. In fact, it's often the little things that indicate recovery. Like the flowers you plant in your garden, recovery will eventually bloom. You can't force flowers to grow; they'll just emerge when they're ready. You must not overwater them or totally neglect them, but you don't have to work hard, either, to draw them out. The same is true for recovery.

In short, recovery takes place slowly and in small increments. It's never a steady process. However, you'll gradually realize that your anxiety, pain, and depression are diminishing. You'll start to have longer and longer periods of inner calm, peace, and serenity. When difficult feelings arise—as they surely will from time to time—their intensity and duration will be less severe than before. You may or may not forget the past, but the feelings associated with your loss will become more manageable and less anxiety-provoking when they do occur.

Signs of Recovery

When Maureen started recovering from her divorce, many things started to change. She noticed that friends and family enjoyed talking to her more and returned her phone calls much more quickly than before. She felt more energy and less fatigue. She started socializing and became more involved in community activities, including volunteer work at her daughter's school. She felt a desire to go back to school and advance her education. All these issues had been difficult for her during the middle phase of her grief process. She also found new confidence and security in her abilities to function in the world. She became more ambitious and outgoing, and she faced her new life with a great deal of strength, courage, and confidence.

Maureen's experiences are characteristic of what people undergo during the late stages of dealing with loss. In keeping with this pattern, the following are the most typical signs of recovery, which we'll explore one by one:

▲ You begin to feel calmer and more accepting of yourself and your situation.
▲ Your concentration improves; you feel more focused.
▲ You feel less depressed and despairing; you're able to enjoy life and pleasurable activities again.
▲ Your daily activities become easier and more enjoyable.
▲ You feel better physically.
▲ Your isolation diminishes, and your social life resumes.
▲ You begin to think about a new career, new projects, or other new commitments.
▲ You begin to find new friends or potential partners.
▲ You take more interest in your appearance.
▲ You begin to feel more at ease with yourself, and you become less self-critical.

You Begin to Feel Calmer and More Accepting of Yourself and Your Situation

You find yourself thinking and talking about your loss less often. This discovery doesn't mean that you feel calm and accepting 100 percent of the time, but the pattern is now more favorable than before. Your emotional state becomes more stable, neither too high nor too low.

It's important that you monitor how much you think about your situation, especially regarding conversations about your loss with friends and family. As you begin to recover, you feel less anxious; you feel calmer, more at peace with yourself. You spend less time obsessing and worrying about the person, relationship, or job you've lost.

Your emotional state is more balanced. It's neither down in the dumps nor totally exhilarated, neither overly optimistic nor excessively pessimistic. You're able to benefit from the good memories you have without idealizing the past. At the same time, you're not fixated on the negative experiences you're starting to transcend.

Celia, for example, felt deeply depressed following her separation from Derek, her longtime lover. The depression continued for so long that she worried that she would never "dig her way out" and feel happy again. Celia confronted her loss, however, and started recovering after many months of soul-searching and intermittent psychotherapy. One sign of recovery was her sense of impatience with her own preoccupations. Among the changes she perceived in her life was simply an eagerness to move on. She continued to miss Derek, but she grew tired of focusing on his absence to the exclusion of other aspects of life. Celia's impatience became a creative force—both a sign of her progress and an impetus toward recovery itself.

What these changes suggest is that you're putting the loss to rest. You find yourself able to see the whole picture—both the good and the bad—and you accept the reality of the loss while simultaneously considering how you benefited from this relationship or job. You're no longer seeing what happened as black or white. There are shades of gray, too, and you're aware of these areas now.

Your Concentration Improves; You Feel More Focused

As you recover, you start to feel much more focused; your thinking is sharper. You're less preoccupied with yourself, hence freer to concentrate some emotional energy on other areas of your life. Your judgment is better, and you feel less confused, less fragmented, and more centered and focused.

You Feel Less Depressed and Despairing; You're Able to Enjoy Life and Pleasurable Activities Again

You start to feel that you've suffered enough; you deserve to be happy again. This attitude may seem self-centered or selfish, but in actuality what you're manifesting is healthy self-love. You feel more entitled or deserving, more worthy of having a good life. You're less likely to turn your anger inward. As you start feeling better and less depressed, you can express your anger and your disappointment over the loss; as the anger wells up openly, you can enjoy life much more than before.

Your Daily Activities Become Easier and More Enjoyable
As you begin to recover, you'll notice that some activities you once found overwhelming, such as doing the laundry or performing other daily tasks, now become more bearable. You're able to do what needs to be done; these tasks don't feel so exhausting. You may even look forward to getting back to these regular activities now that you're less preoccupied with your own sadness and grief.

You may also find that life seems less ponderous now; you don't feel the heavy sense of melancholy you felt before. You laugh more easily. You may begin to find that you have a revived interest in reading the newspaper, listening to the radio, watching news programs. You may find, too, that your conversations with people will be less centered on your own life, perhaps expanding to consider local, national, and world events. You're much more aware of nature, including ordinary phenomena whose beauty you've been ignoring—a sunset, a rainstorm, the changing seasons. You may start listening to music that you haven't heard recently because you feared that it might make you sad.

Here's an example of this sign of recovery (combined with the preceding two signs) in the case of Julie's loss of a lesbian partner, described in Part II. As noted earlier, Julie felt devastated when Marissa jilted her and took sole custody of the couple's son, Max. Julie struggled with the consequences of her loss for several years. Among the difficulties she faced were depression, self-blame, disorganized thinking, and problems in accomplishing daily tasks, both at work and at home. Julie's efforts to deal with her loss paid off in the long run, however. She eventually felt better, both physically and in other ways. Her chronic depression eased. She found her thoughts gradually less chaotic and obsessive. She managed to regain control of her professional and personal activities. She interacted less angrily with Marissa. None of these changes was dramatic or sudden; rather, Julie experienced her recovery as incremental, almost imperceptible. But change did occur. And Julie ultimately found even small changes encouraging, too, since they all seemed part of a larger shift that soon became unstoppable.

You Feel Better Physically

You have more energy when your depression lifts. Exercising seems more enjoyable than before, and you look forward to physical activity again. Starting to exercise leads in turn to greater stamina, which then boosts your capacity for still greater activity.

You're beginning to fall asleep as easily as before your loss, and you sleep through the night without waking. You wake up feeling fine now, not so frightened and alone. You're able to get on with the day—to get up, get dressed, and get going.

Your eating patterns, too, begin to stabilize. During depression, some people tend to overeat while others undereat. Either extreme can be hazardous. But now you're returning to your normal patterns. If you've been overeating, you now eat more moderately. If you've not been eating adequately, you'll begin to see your appetite return. Food starts to taste good again. You regain an interest in taking care of your nutritional needs. You may find that you're eating out less or grabbing fast food less and that you're taking much better care of yourself in that regard; you're preparing meals yourself, perhaps even cooking again if you've done so in the past. In taking care of yourself, you're starting to come back to life, to feel worthy, to nurture yourself again.

One example involves Megan. Megan suffered acute insomnia following the collapse of her relationship with Jacqueline, her older sister. Even when she managed to fall asleep, she often awoke too early, sometimes around 3 or 4 A.M., and couldn't get back to sleep again. Disrupted sleep patterns are a common part of the grief process. Megan, like most people, found that her insomnia diminished over time.

In another example, Leslie engaged in compulsive eating in the aftermath of her divorce—a binge-purge pattern that had occurred during other high-stress times of her life. Leslie recognized this behavior as a significant warning sign, given her past experiences. The help of a sympathetic counselor, combined with the passage of time, ultimately led to less frequent binge-purge eating. Leslie's pattern of eating has now returned to normal.

Your Isolation Diminishes, and Your Social Life Resumes
When you're grieving, you may not want to interact with other people. One of the hardest parts of grieving is tolerating the company of family and friends in certain social situations—the school PTA or PTO, synagogue or church functions, family gatherings, holidays, and birthday parties. Under these circumstances, social occasions can be difficult. People ask you how you are, which seems tedious despite their good intentions, and you may feel a heightened sense of loss around other couples. If you've lost your job, being in a social situation with friends and family may be awkward because people keep asking, "Have you found a job yet?" or "What are you doing about your job search?" and so forth. In short, you may feel pressured while around close family and friends. People mean well, but their questions often intensify rather than alleviate your anxiety.

Once the recovery process is under way, however, you're able to socialize again. You can be around couples without feeling sad—you don't see yourself as half a person any more, but rather as a single person who's doing well and enjoying life. Being with friends and family isn't as taxing as before. You actually begin to enjoy yourself in these situations; later, when your recovery is more advanced, you may even begin to look forward to social gatherings and become more involved with actual planning and preparations.

You Begin to Think About a New Career, New Projects, or Other New Commitments
You may begin to feel as though you have the energy, the time, and the self-worth to attempt new projects or to further your education

and career. You're open to new possibilities. You aren't so fixated and worried about keeping everything the same; you become more adventurous. You begin to perceive the world as a place to explore rather than as a place to endure.

This situation can be especially striking for women. Many women who go through a divorce or career change start to feel empowered. They realize that they are their own person. They discover their own womanhood and their own autonomy as adults, and they realize the power within their grasp. The variety of choices ahead no longer feels like a burden but starts to feel like a gift. They recognize that they are in the driver's seat; they control more choices than they'd thought possible. They start to discover who they really are—what they like and dislike, what they want and don't want, what they need and don't need. Whereas before they may have always acquiesced to a partner, they now find their own sense of self. These changes can be challenging, but they can also lead to a time of tremendous exploration and growth.

A good example that combines this sign of recovery with the previous sign would be Lucinda, whose difficult experiences I described in Part II. Lucinda experienced the loss of both her husband and her son, Bruce. Later, she regained sporadic contact with Bruce. She also remarried and raised another child. Nothing can undo the damage done by her early losses; nevertheless, Lucinda managed to rebuild her life in several important ways. The gradual subsiding of grief led to new relationships and eventually to a second family. Lucinda also pursued a new career—part-time work in a legal office—that allows her both some professional freedom and some flexibility in spending time with her young daughter.

You Begin to Find New Friends or Potential Partners
Finding new friends or love partners doesn't generally happen until you've worked through many of your past patterns of behavior. It's a sign that you're concluding the recovery process. When you begin to choose new friends—friends who are more suitable emotionally,

socially, and intellectually—it shows that you're acting on the insights you've reached about unproductive relationships in your past. After you've completed your own personal journey—whether by means of psychotherapy, self-analysis, involvement in a support group, or something else—you begin to meet new potential partners who are more emotionally available to you than those in the past. One especially good sign is when you choose partners who are kind, considerate, respectful, caring people with good self-esteem—people who are capable of real give-and-take in a relationship. You look for more equitable sharing in your relationships, not situations in which one person dominates and the other submits. You seek relationships in which you can actually share the authority and decision making and in which both partners contribute to each other's emotional, social, intellectual, and economic well-being.

You Take More Interest in Your Appearance
You feel more in touch with your appearance in the wider world. Although it's easy to dismiss this issue as superficial, it's significant in several ways.

First, concern about your appearance is a sign of your accepting yourself and treating yourself well. You feel better when you take care of your body, which in turn influences both your external looks and your internal state of being.

Second, this concern is important as an aspect of your own health and fitness. You start to pay more attention to how you're feeling and looking. As noted earlier, you exercise more, eat appropriately, and take more interest in personal grooming—your hair, your skin, and your attire. Perhaps you haven't really given much attention to how you've been dressing. Whether you're a man or woman, you start looking at your clothes more closely, perhaps shopping for a few new outfits or else attending to issues of personal grooming more than before. This heightened attention to your appearance reflects a greater sense of self-esteem, which in turn influences how others respond to you.

You Begin to Feel More at Ease with Yourself, and You Become Less Self-Critical

This step goes along with increased self-esteem, and your self-esteem in turn puts you still further at ease. You are more accepting of your own and others' imperfections. When you have the ability to laugh at your own imperfections and mistakes, you know you've come a long way. You've really begun to make significant internal changes in your character development, and the presence of change is starting to become more evident in all respects.

This sign of recovery is the inner equivalent of the outer manifestation tagged You Take More Interest in Your Appearance. Both suggest renewed self-acceptance. Ted, whose love affair with Beth (described in Step 1, "Understanding the Nature of Loss") ended as a consequence of parental pressure, went through a period of personal neglect during his initial depression. He dressed sloppily, didn't bother to shave, and ignored his health. Although his appearance improved as the depression eased, active efforts to "clean up his act," as Ted put it, led to inward improvement, too. Self-acceptance and a sense of connection with the world (including a socially acceptable appearance) were interrelated.

One important part of becoming more at ease and less self-critical is that you become gentler toward yourself. You're less likely to blame yourself in a harsh, critical, judgmental way. Instead, you look at your mistakes and losses, you see them as opportunities for growth, and you try to decide what you can learn from your experiences. This flexibility suggests that authentic healing is under way. Some of what you learn may be difficult to admit and accept; from this process of healing, however, you begin to realize that perhaps you did project certain emotions onto others in the past and perhaps you did make some mistakes along the way. Mistakes are simply human. You may have caused some of these problems unconsciously, and you may have caused some pain and suffering for yourself and others. When you can accept your humanity and your imperfections, however, you begin to face your mistakes in an honest, direct manner. And after you're able to face the ghosts from your past, you will then be able to prioritize what is most meaningful in your life.

What is the most important thing in your life? What is the most sacred and the most important essence of your being? When you can answer these questions, you'll have a greater sense of ease, serenity, and peace, and you'll feel much calmer and better about who you are and where you're going. In doing so, you will have come through the recovery process to a much higher level of developmental maturation.

Signs of Stalled Recovery

Although working through the aftermath of loss is difficult and often painful, it's a normal process that most people accomplish without major problems. Most people will see signs of recovery along the lines of those we've discussed in this chapter. In some cases, however, difficulties may arise, warranting concern. Among these difficulties are

- ▲ protracted inability to believe that the loss has occurred
- ▲ protracted social isolation
- ▲ inability to care for yourself
- ▲ reliance on alcohol or drugs to relieve a sense of anguish
- ▲ great effort to avoid thinking about the other person
- ▲ substantial weight gain or loss or deterioration of health
- ▲ suicidal thoughts or gestures or attempted suicide
- ▲ inability to "get on with life" or to invest energy in living

I'll discuss these warning signs one by one.

Protracted Inability to Believe That the Loss Has Occurred

As I've stated elsewhere in this book, shock and disbelief are a normal part of grief, particularly in the initial stages. However, these reactions are normal *only* in the early stages of grief. Protracted inability to accept the reality of a loss is another matter entirely.

This kind of denial often occurs if you feel some kind of fantasy bond with the other person or situation. Fantasies of this sort may happen in response to a childhood situation in which you felt that one or both of your parents didn't care for you or weren't emotionally available. As a result, you hang on to the belief that your loss hasn't really happened. You may also have idealized the other person in some way. If so, there's a deeper, more complicated problem that keeps you in a state of disbelief or denial. You deny reality because it's less painful for you to pretend that the loss hasn't occurred.

If you're in this state of denial or disbelief, what should you do? Protracted denial or disbelief—lasting longer than, say, six months or so—may well start affecting your life and your normal functioning. Under these circumstances, it's important to get psychological help—counseling, psychotherapy, or help from a support group. Past experiences can keep you from accepting the reality of what's going on in your life, and this situation can significantly harm your day-to-day existence and future happiness.

Protracted Social Isolation

In the aftermath of loss, you're probably not feeling good about yourself. You're feeling weak or vulnerable. You're also feeling that you need time to withdraw for a while—to process what has happened, to think, to cry and scream and yell. Withdrawal of this sort is generally fine, a normal part of grieving. However, social isolation shouldn't last for a protracted period. Six months to a year would be the longest I'd suggest for this isolated state.

In Part I, I mentioned Jamie, the gifted young lawyer whose conflicted relationship with her father contributed to various troubled love affairs. Jamie has managed to gain control of her life in many ways, but the individual losses she has suffered have often led to periods of severe depression. Among her difficulties are refusal to acknowledge the reality of loss and, on several occasions, withdrawal from life to an alarming degree. Her withdrawing isn't brief or partial; at times it's total—a complete severing of social and professional ties. Jamie has lost two jobs as a consequence, and she has alienated many of her friends. Fortunately, she now recognizes the risks of this behavior, perceives it as a warning sign, and generally responds by seeking psychiatric help.

Isolation can be advantageous to grieving for a while; if it's too long, however, the state tends to be self-perpetuating. One possibility is clinical depression. If this occurs, you need help—psychological intervention, perhaps including the use of antidepressant medication. If your isolation lasts longer than six to eight months, you should investigate the symptoms you're experiencing. *Again, I'm not referring to temporary, early-stage withdrawal.* When isolation is protracted, however, it tends to be detrimental.

Inability to Care for Yourself

Another significant concern is an inability or disinterest in performing day-to-day activities. Not taking care of yourself, not getting out of bed in the morning, not functioning well at work, not interacting effectively with coworkers, not being able to do the laundry, go shopping, cook a meal, take care of your home, or get your kids to school—any problem along these lines is worrisome. Other areas of concern are not exercising, overeating, undereating, and neglecting basic hygiene. Of course we all have days when it's tempting to stay in bed rather than face the world, and there's nothing wrong with taking an occasional "mental health day." But a brief break from responsibility isn't the issue here. I'm talking about a fundamental ability to function. On the other hand, racing around in a manic state warrants attention, too. You should be concerned about extremes either way.

Why are these day-to-day matters important? On one level, it's just a question of practicality: you need to keep yourself (not to mention your kids) fed, housed, and healthy. On another level, these issues are also the outward signs of your inward well-being. If you can't function, you've lost at least a degree of your will to live. It's not that you're actively self-destructive; rather, you're neglecting yourself in a passive but still troubling way. You've slumped to a lower level of functioning. If you feel you're unable to care for yourself and your children, you should seek immediate professional attention.

Reliance on Alcohol or Drugs to Relieve a Sense of Anguish

If you're using drink or drugs to numb your pain or boost your mood, you may end up severely complicating your problems. Substance abuse isn't an uncommon response to grief, and in some ways it's an understandable—though always dangerous—reaction. Alcohol and drugs can provide an illusion of control and comfort. Unfortunately, the illusion is short-lived. Drugs and alcohol may help you feel better temporarily, but you'll often feel even worse when the effects wear off.

Jared, rejected by his wife, responded to his loss by protracted drinking. In the past, he had used alcohol both to numb his pain and to "cry for help." This time, however, his wife refused to answer. Jared drank so heavily that he suffered a serious fall, cutting his face; confronted by hospital personnel about his drinking, he entered an Alcoholics Anonymous program and is now gaining control of the situation.

If you're relying on drugs or alcohol to keep going or to bolster your self-confidence, you should seek professional help as soon as possible. Don't tell yourself that confronting this issue means you're weak; on the contrary, you're being strong to admit you have a problem. We can all benefit from others' help. We're all struggling to understand the complexities of life. If you can be gentle with yourself and if you can recognize when you're in trouble, accepting the possibility of help can be easier. In addition to psychotherapy, resources include many useful support groups such as Alcoholics Anonymous, Narcanon, and others. (See Appendix A for a detailed listing.)

Great Effort to Avoid Thinking About the Other Person

If you spend a lot of your time, attention, and energy thinking about or talking about your loss, you may be struggling with what psychologists call an *obsessive neurosis*. It's possible that you're avoiding the tasks of recovery through your preoccupation with the past. It's understandable that your loss has a major place in your thoughts. At the same time, obsessive thoughts—especially if they focus on controlling other people's behavior—keep you in a state of confusion. Obsessive thoughts also keep you from focusing on yourself, your own feelings, and your needs during a time of loss. When you're obsessed with someone else, you're abandoning your own self in some respects. This, too, may warrant professional attention.

Substantial Weight Gain or Loss or Deterioration of Health

Feeling abused or abandoned can trigger a terrible sense of loss. At the same time, it can create a sense of outrage at your lack of control over the situations you face. Some people respond to this situation by eating more or less food or by exercising more or less. Why? Because eating and exercise are ways by which they can feel a sense of control. However, this kind of control can be paradoxical and counterproductive. You may be able to control the amount of food you put into your mouth, and bingeing (or fasting) may grant you a sense of power. The truth is, though, that the power isn't what it seems. The paradox is that you're out of control precisely when you're overeating. You're out of control when you're starving yourself. These behaviors create a false sense of control because whatever you may be doing externally, you are internally out of control.

It's not just a question of food. What is out of control is *anger*. You may feel that if you release your anger, the experience will be so painful that you'll lose control. Because these feelings can be so intense and worrisome, you may attempt to control your external reality—your weight, your diet, your appearance. But this effort doesn't address the real issues. And until you do so, whether alone or with professional help, you're likely to feel that things remain out of control.

Suicidal Thoughts or Gestures or Attempted Suicide

When you're suffering from a major loss, suicidal thoughts aren't unusual. Protracted or intense suicidal thoughts, however, can be a cause for concern. If these thoughts impede your everyday functioning, it's time to seek outside help.

Many of these thoughts relate to unresolved or unfinished business from your past. The more problems you faced before your loss and the more unfinished business or unresolved issues existed before the loss, the longer the duration and intensity of grief reactions.

Abandoned by her husband, Marti struggled both with her sense of emotional devastation and with the practical tasks of raising two children alone. Marti felt so overwhelmed that she sometimes wondered how she could keep on living. She would pass an open window and fantasize about jumping out; she would see a bottle of sleeping pills and imagine taking them; she would experience other suicidal impulses. Down deep, Marti believed that she would never kill herself—not with a young son and daughter who depended on her. But the fantasies would flicker through her mind all the same, frightening her.

It's important to distinguish between suicidal thoughts and actual gestures or attempts. It's not unusual to have an occasional suicidal thought or feeling; when those suicidal thoughts become constant or pervasive, however, or when you start planning to take your life or even make a serious attempt, you should seek immediate professional assistance. Locate a therapist, counselor, or support group. And if you feel you'll act on your suicidal impulses, call a suicide prevention hot line at once. (Check your local phone directory; if you can't find appropriate services quickly, dial 911 or your community's emergency response number.)

Inability to "Get on with Life" or to Invest Energy in Living
Melancholy or low energy are common aspects of a broken heart. Everyone has a right to feel disappointed by loss and to step back from habitual activities as a way of regaining a sense of balance. When these feelings are protracted, however—when they last longer than about six months or a year or when they undermine your everyday life and ability to function—then you probably need professional help.

Many of us can function under the influence of low-level depression. Some people carry this burden for years. But when it obstructs your ability to get on with life; to perform your daily tasks; or to pursue your career, friendships, and parental obligations—that's another matter. There's particular concern when this state of mind interferes with your obligations as a parent. If you've suffered a loss, your kids will pick up on your state of mind even if you're not aware of it yourself. It's not always possible to "pull yourself up by your bootstraps." Denying your condition won't solve your problems, and you may start to perceive signs and symptoms in your children or other people who depend on you. As in other situations we've discussed, this should prompt you to seek professional help. Your behavior affects not only you but the people around you—your friends, your family, your children, your loved ones, your colleagues at work, and perhaps others as well. Don't expect your family and friends to carry your burden. At the same time, don't try to carry it alone. Seek help from someone with training and objectivity who can assist you in your journey without becoming enmeshed in your problems.

Other Warning Signs

The list of warning signs I've discussed here isn't intended to be comprehensive or categorical. All sorts of issues can arise and affect your state of mind or behavior, and people differ greatly in what seems problematic or normal. So you shouldn't take anything I've said here as carved in stone. In closing, though, here are a few other issues that can suggest problematic recovery from a loss:

▲ prolonged fatigue—feeling listless, lacking energy, or sleeping for long, long periods of time

▲ protracted or excessive use of over-the-counter medication for headaches, stomachaches, back pain, flu, colds, or other physical symptoms

▲ an inability to slow down—that is, a state of mania or hyperactivity, in which you engage in frenzied activity to distract yourself from disturbing emotions or thoughts

▲ protracted inability to focus or to concentrate or think clearly or protracted feelings of confusion or anxiety

▲ protracted inability to assert yourself or a sense of being overwhelmed by fears and doubts

▲ feelings of severely diminished self-esteem with exaggerated concerns about what other people may be thinking about you

▲ for women, severely disrupted menstrual periods, with or without an increase in premenstrual difficulties

▲ inability to maintain friendships or other relationships

▲ extreme negativity or pessimism regardless of external circumstances

▲ an exaggerated sense of guilt, self-blame, self-doubt, often accompanied by diminished self-esteem and self-worth

Thinking Positive

As you read over the preceding discussions, each of which outlines a different warning sign, it's possible that you feel growing concern and anxiety. Are you too depressed, too withdrawn, too overwhelmed, too anxious, too this, or too that? Please keep in mind that this overview isn't intended to alarm you; rather, it's a sketch of potential problems, most or all of which are unlikely to affect any one individual. I urge you *not* to review these issues in a way that makes you hypersensitive to what you're feeling. Think positive! The truth is, most people deal with loss in a constructive way; it's probable that you will, too.

My intention in this chapter is simply to provide a way of sizing up your state of mind as you work your way toward recovery. For most people, the signs of recovery that make up the first half of this chapter are more relevant than the signs of stalled recovery that follow. Even the warning signs are not cause for panic. They are just a series of signposts that can indicate if you have strayed off course.

If you truly feel that your state of mind is problematic, however, it's important not to delay before seeking help. Don't let your health deteriorate. Don't suffer extreme stress without some kind of safe release. Don't allow your kids to suffer the side effects of your loss. Don't "go it alone" when you can benefit from a trained guide's help. You can take preventive measures before the damage is unavoidable. And even if you feel totally bogged down in your problems, it's never too late to start over. If you don't know where to turn, start with Appendix A, "Information and Support Groups," which is full of useful resources.

What to Remember About Step 5: Becoming Aware of Your Recovery

▲ The grief process is erratic—often two steps forward, one step back.

▲ However, you will gradually perceive signs of your recovery such as these:

△ You begin to feel calmer and more accepting of yourself and your situation.

△ Your concentration improves; you feel more focused.

△ You feel less depressed and despairing; you're able to enjoy life and pleasurable activities again.

△ Your daily activities become easier and more enjoyable.

△ You feel better physically.

△ Your isolation diminishes, and your social life resumes.

△ You begin to think about a new career, new projects, or other new commitments.

△ You begin to find new friends or potential partners.

△ You take more interest in your appearance.

△ You begin to feel more at ease with yourself, and you become less self-critical.

▲ Most people experience these signs of recovery. In some cases, however, difficulties arise, such as these:

△ protracted inability to believe that the loss has occurred

△ protracted social isolation

△ inability to care for yourself

△ reliance on alcohol or drugs to relieve a sense of anguish

△ great effort to avoid thinking of the other person

△ substantial weight gain or loss or deterioration of health

△ suicidal thoughts or gestures or attempted suicide

△ inability to "get on with life" or to invest energy in living

▲ Despite these risks, it's important to think positive. Most people deal with loss constructively.

STEP 6

*A*ccepting Progress, Not Perfection

Since happily-ever-after expectations wreak so much havoc on relationships, what's the alternative? The answer is the final step of our six-step process, accepting imperfection. By this I mean *the ability to perceive your own development as a continuous state of change rather than as the attainment of an idealized goal.* The value of having this ability may seem obvious, even elementary. Most people, however, are hostage to a belief that they should be perfect. Yet only by accepting the uncertainties and unpredictabilities of being human can you move beyond loss and embrace people—including yourself—for what they really are. In short, you need to be guided by reality, not by fantasy.

Accepting progress rather than perfection doesn't mean that you cease to have dreams. Rather, it means that you start to see dreams as inspirations, not as a solid place or permanent state that you expect to reach. There's no harm in dreaming of a wonderful relationship if you accept both yourself and the other person as complex, ambivalent, unpredictable, and flawed human beings and if you can commit yourself to working through the ordinary ups and downs of human interactions.

Reality-Based Relationships

Throughout this book, I've offered examples of relationships that suffered from unrealistic expectations. Here, now, are examples of the alternatives—reality-based relationships between people who have learned to accept progress, not perfection.

Lisa and Daren

A divorced social worker with two children, Lisa assumed that she would never remarry. Her experience of marriage had been a disaster; she felt no desire to go through that ordeal again. At the age of forty-five, she felt lonely but resigned to living the rest of her life without a mate.

Then she met a man named Daren. Nothing remarkable happened between them initially; they just chatted at a singles club, danced for a while, and exchanged phone numbers. A few get-togethers followed in the ensuing weeks. Though physically attracted to each other, they established a relationship that seemed cordial and curious rather than romantic. Daren, too, had been divorced. Both he and Lisa felt wary of intense involvement, and both had children: Lisa, two; Daren, five. Life seemed complex enough without the added complications of a major love affair.

Ultimately, Daren and Lisa chose to become more involved, but they took six years to integrate their relationship. They proceeded with great caution. Both had undergone psychotherapy; both had reached a point where they understood the dynamics of their respective families. They concentrated on getting to know each other without putting themselves or their kids in a difficult situation. They worked hard to keep their developing relationship separate from the kids, since they knew that children—especially children who have suffered through a divorce—can be traumatized by parents' hasty attachment to a new partner. As they grew close over the years, however, and as they made a stronger commitment to each other, Lisa and Daren got to know each other's children, and they stabilized the two families' interactions.

Their careers also provided a number of challenges. Daren, a computer engineer, unexpectedly lost his job. Although he found new work eventually, the loss of the earlier position and the rigors of his subsequent job search proved stressful. Lisa's work, too, was demanding. The couple went through many ups and downs as they grew close. They didn't by any means experience a fantasy or fairy-tale relationship; Lisa and Daren confronted many difficulties, including uncertainties over what kind of future they wanted. But as they got to know each other better and spent more time on a day-to-day basis, Lisa and Daren formed a truly strong bond.

Meanwhile, the children took years to adjust to the changes that Daren's and Lisa's relationship created. Trouble arose over stepparenting styles, sibling conflicts, money problems, and many other issues. Nothing came easily to either partner or to any of their kids. There were lots of frustrating, difficult moments. Both Lisa and Daren worked incredibly hard to stay patient with the tasks before them. Everyone involved had to compromise and negotiate. Daren and Lisa took the process slowly, however, and let everyone in both families adjust on a gradual basis.

Ultimately, Lisa and Daren got married. It has now been two years since the wedding. The kids from both families get along well together, and (despite some predictable ups and downs) they enjoy each other's company. Daren and Lisa are emotionally close. Life is strenuous, but almost everything is going well enough to inspire confidence. Those aspects that remain difficult—and inevitably there are plenty—seem well within the couple's ability to cope.

Joan and Ben

Joan, married for less than a year to her "dream husband," felt crushed when the man she considered Mr. Perfect ran off with a former girlfriend. She mourned the loss of her marriage but also felt humiliated by the bursting of her illusions. She suspected that she'd rectify the situation quickly, though; she'd find someone better than her first husband.

After several years of dating men, however—getting involved quickly and intensely and then suffering yet another loss within a few weeks or months—Joan knew that she had a problem. She just kept repeating the same old mistakes. Almost invariably she picked men who were handsome, sexy, and financially well-off but ultimately unresponsive to her emotional needs. Joan couldn't understand why she kept linking up with the same kind of remote, manipulative guy. By means of psychotherapy, though, she gradually understood the reasons for her choices, and she learned to be more selective about possible partners.

Some years ago, Joan answered a personal ad placed by a man named Ben. She knew at once that he was very different from the people she'd been attracted to in the past. At first she felt uneasy. Ben wasn't the glamorous, charming, high-powered sort of man that she'd always felt drawn to. He was a college professor, thirty-eight years old, divorced, with no children from his previous marriage. He wasn't especially attractive, charismatic, or charming. If anything, he was excessively modest and shy. At the same time, Ben was kind, interesting, and affectionate. The relationship that soon developed was calm and comfortable. Despite Joan's initial skepticism, she found herself drawn to Ben in a relaxed, unpressured way. This wasn't a fantasy relationship, but it seemed solid and comfortable.

Joan and Ben felt lucky and appreciative to have found each other. They shared many interests, beliefs, and values, and they enjoyed similar activities; yet they were different from one another, too, which added spice to their interactions. Both their similarities and differences forged a strong bond. Joan felt that despite her initial reservations, she had finally found a man who would treat her with respect and stable affection. Ben, too, seemed to appreciate Joan as a person. Not long ago, they got married.

For his birthday—the first birthday that they've celebrated as husband and wife—Joan bought Ben a pair of running shoes. She knew how much Ben loves running. Because this was a different kind of gift from what she'd been accustomed to giving, however, she initially felt uncomfortable with her choice. It was so practical, so everyday. All the same, Ben loved the gift. In many ways the shoes seemed so *right*, a fitting symbol of their good, comfortable relationship.

Al and Luke

For almost ten years, Al lived with his lover, Michael, in Boston. Al perceived his relationship with Michael as imbalanced and unpredictable, but it suited his professional ambitions, for Michael's success as a commercial realtor allowed Al complete financial freedom to pursue his artistic career. The lovers were very different: Michael was driven, materialistic, and outgoing; Al was introverted and indifferent to worldly success. Al tolerated the stresses he felt, hoping that he and Michael would sort things out eventually. At some point, however, Al realized that he was mostly just another item in Michael's collection of beautiful things. The relationship soon dissolved.

Al struggled with the aftermath of this loss for many years. He missed Michael yet seethed at how his lover had "kept" him and condescended to him. Psychotherapy helped. Al started to see how his family background (not to mention his struggles as a gay man in an often hostile society) had shaped his behavior. But he still felt lonely and confused.

Meeting Luke was a turning point. Luke, though a hospital bureaucrat by profession, was a gifted amateur artist and deeply appreciative of Al's own talents. Even their initial conversations brought tears to Al's eyes; here was someone who supported his artistic pursuits because he appreciated art, not because having Al around made him feel sophisticated. The two men became immediate friends. They considered living together but quickly decided to hold off. Al felt leery of having anyone bankroll his life again. He thought it was better to take it slow, to live independently at first, exploring their relationship before exerting more strain on it than it might tolerate.

Al and Luke benefited from this slow approach, for both men needed time to understand each other and themselves. Both had struggled for a long time with the societal consequences of being gay. Both had worked hard to resolve conflicts with their respective families. Both had experienced painful earlier relationships—Al with Michael, Luke with his ex-wife, who was still troubled by Luke's homosexuality. After tackling these issues separately, Luke and Al decided to enter therapy together. A psychotherapist who specializes in couples therapy for gay men helped them understand the past and, ultimately, the future.

My sense is that Luke and Al have a good relationship ahead of them. They have a stable, loving bond; they have lost most of their illusions about the task of living together; and they share many interests and values. Both men still struggle with a sense of loss from the past. Luke, especially, has a complex set of demands to face from Lucinda, his daughter by his ex-wife. Yet both Al and Luke are working hard, they love each other, and they've ceased to see their relationship as something that will happen without forethought, effort, and imagination.

Jenny and Marie

Jenny, three years younger than Marie, was always intensely jealous of her older sister. Jenny looked up to Marie yet considered her self-centered, narcissistic, and overly ambitious, while Jenny tended to be introverted and withdrawn. Though talented, Jenny suffered from low self-esteem. During their childhood, Marie had helped Jenny a lot, with the older sister parenting the younger to a great degree. There was intense sibling rivalry all along, however. Their adult years have been difficult as well; when Marie went through a divorce, she grew tired of having a quasi-parental role toward Jenny, who expected a lot yet never gave much in return.

Recently, the situation has started to improve. Marie's ongoing therapy has helped her recognize her role in the family—a role that was unrealistic and frustrating for both women—and she has managed to reject her old fantasy of what sisters are supposed to be. Among other things, Marie grasps how much of this situation their parents (especially their mother) set up. The mother didn't have sisters herself. She had created a fantasy of what sister love was supposed to be and had communicated that fantasy to her daughters. This and other family dynamics had greatly complicated the sisters' lives. In many ways, they didn't really know how to relate to each other as women, and a sense of rivalry created by their mother had filtered down to them. It took many years for Jenny and Marie to understand each other, to accept each other as they really were, and to mature as individuals.

Even now, their relationship isn't consistently communicative. Jenny is still going through many changes, and she hasn't reached some of the insights that Marie has. Love exists between them, however. There is new communication based much more nearly on reality than before. The sisters are able to express their discontents, anger, sadness, and affection. Their relationship is now consistently based much more on reality.

Crisis or Opportunity?

The sense of loss that most people feel when a cherished relationship ends usually creates a personal crisis. At best, there's a sense of disorientation and disappointment. At worst, there's a feeling that the world has ended. The steps I've described throughout *How to Mend a Broken Heart* probably suggest that the grief process following a major loss is intense, difficult, and complex. It is. I won't

pretend otherwise. Neither will I claim that my suggestions for coping with this process will take away all your pain and solve all your
problems. The truth is that your loss—whether it's the end of a marriage, a love affair, a sibling bond, a job, or something else—is probably a major life crisis. By its nature, this kind of crisis makes great
demands on you, including the difficult task of perceiving other people—and yourself as well—in new ways.

Yet as is often true, this kind of crisis is also an opportunity—
perhaps even a cluster of opportunities. Perceiving other people in
new ways offers you the opportunity to create new relationships and
to deepen old ones. Perceiving yourself in new ways offers you the
opportunity for insight, growth, and wisdom. Like all human beings,
you have a nearly unlimited capacity for change and development.
Struggles with loss and grief, though painful, usually lead to a
deeper, fuller appreciation of life and of your individual place within
the human community.

The key to making crisis into opportunity is accepting progress,
not perfection. Take the challenge that loss presents to you. Open
your mind, heart, and soul to the possibilities that life offers you.
Dare to dream, but see your dreams as starting points for life rather
than as guarantees for what life will become.

What follows are a few final thoughts about loss, the grief
process, and the differences between progress and perfection.

The grief process is complex, ambiguous, and often confusing.
Recovering from a major loss challenges your self-confidence,
patience, insight, and stamina, and you often take two steps forward
and one step back rather than following a steady course.

*Recovering from a significant loss is one of the hardest tasks you'll
ever face.* It takes hard work to get back on your feet again. Recovery demands consistent, strenuous effort to reconnect and reestablish good, stable, solid relationships.

Everything we've described in this book takes time. If you rush the
process, you'll end up complicating the tasks you face, and you may
even take longer to recover than you would otherwise. Try to be open

to your feelings. Instead of fighting your emotions—whether disbelief, shock, anger, sadness, or whatever—embrace them. Feel what you're feeling.

Accepting progress means acknowledging that you haven't "arrived." This realization is hard for most people to tolerate; in fact, many find it unbearable. But it's still the nature of human development. Change is inevitable. Although you may find change threatening, life may turn out better, richer, and more exciting if you're open to all the possibilities ahead rather than rigidly attached to a specific outcome or goal. In addition, you'll have your own individual path to find and changes to undergo. And remember, the only time you'll stop changing is when you're dead. Celebrate life!

Although life can present you with many devastating crises, it's up to you to transform each crisis into something else. Turn your crises into opportunities.

Never give up.

PART IV

*R*esources

*T*here is perhaps no greater source of needless frustration during a personal or family crisis than the belief that you're dealing with it entirely alone. Even the most competent adult can be worn down and demoralized by a feeling of isolation. Fortunately, an increasing number of organizations exist to help you with the problems you face. This increase has occurred despite (or because of) the decline of state and federally financed social services in recent years. Admittedly, the task of finding and coordinating available resources takes effort and imagination. But you can find help during your time of need.

This section of *How to Mend a Broken Heart* therefore serves to bring possible resources to your attention.

APPENDIX A

$\mathcal{I}$nformation and Support Groups

In this section, I've categorized listings as carefully as possible; however, some of the organizations' purposes or services overlap. Please check the whole list to make sure you aren't missing a good source of help. Also, note that most of these resources are clearing-houses or umbrella organizations. They won't provide direct services, but they can inform you of specific agencies or groups that offer such services in your community.

Organizations That Offer Information About Various Issues

Aging and Care of the Aging

American Senior Citizens Association (ASCA)
P.O. Box 41
Fayetteville, NC 28302
(919) 323-3641

The ASCA's purpose is "to promote the physical, mental, emotional, and economic well-being of senior citizens."

Children of Aging Parents (CAPS)
Woodbourne Office Campus, Suite 302A
1609 Woodbourne Road
Levittown, PA 19057-1511
(215) 945-6900
(800) CAPS-294

CAPS is an organization that produces and distributes literature for caregivers; offers individual peer counseling in person and by telephone; publishes a newsletter, *The Capsule*; provides employee assistance programs; assists in developing support groups nationally; and maintains ongoing caregiver support groups. Available materials include a bibliography, manuals for starting support groups for caregivers, and information sheets on housing options for the elderly, Medicare, financial management, estate planning, tips for caregivers, and reprints from *The Capsule*.

Jewish Association for Services of the Aged (JASA)
40 W. 68th Street
New York, NY 10023
(212) 724-3200

JASA is a social welfare organization "whose objective is to provide the services necessary to enable the older adult to remain in the community."

National Council on the Aging, Inc. (NCOA)
409 Third Street, S.W.
Washington, DC 20024
(202) 479-1200
(202) 479-6653

The National Council on the Aging serves primarily to inform professional caregivers about research and resources for the elderly. However, some NCOA materials may be useful to families themselves. Among these publications are *Caregiving Tips, Long-Term Care Choices, Respite Resource Guide,* and *Long-Distance Caregiving.*

Support Source
420 Rutgers Avenue
Swarthmore, PA 19081
(215) 544-3605

Support Source publishes *Help for Families of the Aging*, a workbook and leaders' manual for seminars intended to help caregivers of the elderly cope with the tasks facing them.

Alcohol and Substance Abuse

Al-Anon Family Group Headquarters, Inc.
P.O. Box 862, Midtown Station
New York, NY 10018-0862
(212) 302-7240
(800) 356-9996

Al-Anon maintains thirty thousand regional groups that serve relatives and friends of individuals with an alcohol problem. In addition, Al-Anon produces publications, including newsletters, about alcoholism.

Alateen
P.O. Box 862, Midtown Station
New York, NY 10018-0862
(212) 302-7240
(800) 356-9996

Alateen is an organization similar to Al-Anon but focused on helping teenage friends and relatives of persons coping with alcoholism.

Alcoholics Anonymous World Services (A.A.)
475 Riverside Drive
New York, NY 10163
(212) 870-3400

A.A. serves to help members "solve their common problem and help others achieve sobriety through a twelve-step program."

Cocaine Anonymous World Services
3740 Overland Avenue, Suite H
Los Angeles, CA 90034-6337
(310) 559-5833
(800) 347-8998

Cocaine Anonymous is a "fellowship of men and women who share their experiences, strength, and hope" to "solve their common problem and help others recover from addiction and remain free from cocaine and other mind-altering drugs."

Drug-Anon Focus
P.O. Box 20806, Park West Station
New York, NY 10025
(212) 484-9095

Drug-Anon Focus is a self-help support organization for the families and friends of persons addicted to mood-altering drugs.

Families Anon
P.O. Box 3475
Culver City, CA 90231-3475
(310) 313-5800
(800) 736-9805

Families Anon consists of "local groups of parents, relatives, and friends concerned about drug abuse or related behavior problems."

Narcotics Anonymous
P.O. Box 9999
Van Nuys, CA 91409
(818) 773-9999

Through Narcotics Anonymous, "recovering addicts throughout the world meet to offer help to fellow addicts seeking recovery."

National Association for Children of Alcoholics (NACOA)
11426 Rockville Pike, Suite 100
Rockville, MD 20852
(301) 468-0985

NACOA "supports and serves as a resource for individuals of all age groups who are COAs."

National Council on Alcoholism, Inc. (NCA)
12 W. 21st Street
New York, NY 10010
(212) 206-6770

NCA provides information about educational and counseling resources on alcoholism.

Assistance to Women

Older Women's League (OWL)
666 11th Street
Washington, DC 20001
(202) 783-6686

"The Older Women's League is the only national grassroots membership organization whose sole focus is women in the middle years and beyond." Created in 1980, OWL addresses issues such as pension rights, health insurance, and caregiver and support services. OWL publishes a newspaper and a series of workbooks for women's midlife planning.

Women's Action Alliance, Inc.
370 Lexington Avenue, Suite 603
New York, NY 10017
(212) 532-8330
"The Alliance is a national not-for-profit service organization dedicated to realizing the vision of self-determination for all women." Although the Alliance doesn't provide services directly applicable to medical care and bereavement services, it can supply information about agencies that can help women deal with family issues.

Compulsive Gambling

Gam-Anon International Service Office
P.O. Box 157
Whitestone, NY 11357
(718) 352-1671
Gam-Anon "seeks to help members understand the compulsive gambler and to learn to cope with the problems involved."

Gamblers Anonymous
P.O. Box 17173
Los Angeles, CA 90010
(213) 386-8789
Gamblers Anonymous consists of nine hundred local groups to help "men and women who have joined together . . . to stop gambling."

Death and Dying

Accord Aftercare Services
1930 Bishop Lane, Suite 947
Louisville, KY 40218
(800) 346-3087
Organized primarily to provide grief information and materials to professionals who work with the bereaved, Accord Aftercare Services distributes a wide variety of brochures, audiocassettes, and videotapes about loss and grief. In addition, Accord conducts workshops on grief education for professionals.

Center for Death Education and Research (CDER)
Department of Sociology
909 Social Science Building
267 19th Avenue South
University of Minnesota
Minneapolis, MN 55455-0412

CDER sells books, pamphlets, and articles about a wide range of subjects pertaining to death and dying. Although many of these publications are most appropriate for mental health professionals, others are intended for a lay audience.

The Compassionate Friends
P.O. Box 3696
Oak Brook, IL 60522-3696
(630) 990-0010

"The Compassionate Friends is a mutual assistance, self-help organization offering friendship and understanding to bereaved parents. The purposes are to support and aid parents and siblings in the positive resolution of the grief experienced upon the death of their child or brother/sister and to foster the physical and emotional health of bereaved parents and siblings." Available resources include local chapters with support groups for the bereaved, educational services, and an extensive list of books and pamphlets.

Divorce and Child Custody

Divorce Support
5020 W. School Street
Chicago, IL 60641
(773) 286-4541

This Chicago-area group serves people in the region "who are divorced, separated, or experiencing marital problems."

Parents Sharing Custody (PSC)
420 S. Beverly Drive, Suite 100
Beverly Hills, CA 90210-4410
(310) 286-9171

PSC is an "organization for parents sharing custody of children following divorce."

Women Helping Women (WHW)
525 N. Van Buren Street
Stoughton, WI 53589
(608) 873-3747
WHW "offers mutual support and exchange of ideas for those going through the divorce procedure."

Domestic Violence

National Center for Assault Protection (NCAP)
606 Delsea Drive
Sewell, NJ 08080
(609) 582-7000
(800) 258-3189
NCAP's purpose is to prevent interpersonal violence through education, assistance to children, and research into the causes and consequences of violence.

Grandparents

Grandparents Anonymous (GPA)
1924 Beverly
Sylvan Lake, MI 48320
(810) 682-8384
GPA serves to help "grandparents who are denied legal visitation of grandchildren."

Grandparents Raising Grandchildren (GRG)
P.O. Box 104
Colleyville, TX 76034
(817) 577-0435
GRG "provides emotional support, legal assistance, and a unified voice for grandparents seeking to protect and care for their grandchildren."

Health Issues

National Self-Help Clearinghouse
Graduate School and University Center
City University of New York
25 W. 42d Street, Suite 620
New York, NY 10036
(212) 642-2944
    If your loved one suffers from specific illnesses or health conditions, you can obtain information about medical matters and/or available resources from this helpful umbrella organization.

Suicide Prevention and Counseling

American Association of Suicidology (AAS)
4201 Connecticut Avenue, N.W.
Washington, DC 20008
(202) 237-2280
    AAS can supply information about support groups for survivors of suicide, as well as literature about suicide and its aftermath for families. (Note: AAS is an information clearinghouse, *not* a crisis center.)

Ray of Hope
P.O. Box 2323
Iowa City, IA 52244
(319) 337-9890
    Ray of Hope is a self-help organization offering support for coping with suicide, loss, and grief. Services include the selling of publications and videos.

Samaritans
500 Commonwealth Avenue
Kenmore Square
Boston, MA 02215
    This nonreligious group offers information, intervention, and publications regarding suicide.

Widowhood

Widowed Persons Service
American Association of Retired Persons (AARP)
601 E Street, N.W.
Washington, DC 20049
(202) 434-2277

In addition to providing a variety of services to the retired, AARP sponsors a program called Widowed Persons Service. This service offers dozens of local programs nationwide to newly widowed persons of all ages. AARP also provides publications, among them an excellent pamphlet titled *On Being Alone*; a bibliography on bereavement; a list of national and local programs for the widowed; and a catalog of several hundred publications. See also additional listing under Other Resources.

Other Resources

American Association of Retired Persons (AARP)
601 E Street, N.W.
Washington, DC 20049
(202) 434-2277

AARP provides a wide range of services for the retired. This organization's concerns include medical, financial, educational, and safety issues. In addition, AARP has some of the best information available about resources for widows and widowers. (See also additional listing under Widowhood.)

Household International
Corporate Communications
2700 Sanders Road
Prospect Heights, IL 60070
(847) 564-5000

To provide consumers with information about planning, investment, saving, and other financial issues, Household International has produced a series of booklets available at a nominal cost.

National Organization for Victim Assistance (NOVA)
1757 Park Road, N.W.
Washington, DC 20010
(202) 232-6682

NOVA is a private, nonprofit organization providing four services: national advocacy for victims' rights; direct services, including counseling and follow-up assistance for crime victims; professional development of local programs; and membership communication and support. Among other things, NOVA can help you locate victim assistance resources in your community. NOVA also provides a twenty-four-hour telephone crisis line for all types of crime victims.

National Self-Help Clearinghouse (NSHC)
Graduate School and University Center
City University of New York
25 W. 42d Street, Suite 620
New York, NY 10036

NSHC "encourages and conducts training activities, carries out research, maintains a data bank to provide information about self-help groups, and publishes manuals, training materials, and a newsletter." To obtain information about self-help groups throughout the United States, send $1 to the above address.

Parents Without Partners (PWP)
401 N. Michigan Avenue
Chicago, IL 60611-4267
(800) 637-7974

This organization's services could be useful to adults who are attempting to care for their own parents while raising children alone. PWP provides publications and brochures for single parents.

On-Line Information

As in other aspects of contemporary life, computer on-line services have increased your options for obtaining information on any of the issues listed above. That's the good news. The bad news is that the sources of information change often and unpredictably. (Even the means of contacting sources—that is, the particular on-line services for accessing particular databases—are in constant flux.) Because any specific list of resources would be obsolete within a year or two, what follows is simply a general overview of on-line information and how it may help you in dealing with your personal crisis.

On-Line Services

Commercial on-line services often have resources you can access to obtain information or find support. Typical services are databases, bulletin boards, and discussion groups. *Databases* are compilations of data on one or more subjects accessible by computer. *Bulletin boards* are electronic listings of topics, subtopics, and responses. *Discussion groups* (sometimes called *chat rooms*) are real-time interactions between on-line participants. At the time of this writing, for instance, America Online, CompuServe, and Prodigy all have services of these several sorts. For example: within its Baby Boomer area, America Online has message topics that include Dealing with Relationships (and a subtopic for Divorce). CompuServe and Prodigy have similar bulletin boards. In addition, each of these services can provide access to health-related databases with information about specific illnesses, caregiving resources, and other data that you may find useful.

The Internet

You can also find information on the Internet, the "network of networks." Most commercial on-line services provide either limited or complete Internet access; check your users' manual or on-line users' information for details. Alternatively, you can use Internet browsers (software for navigating the Internet) for direct Internet access through Internet Service Providers (ISPs) such as PSI, Netcom, and others. Either way, you can obtain information or join Internet discussion groups on a wide variety of topics. People coping with many illnesses, for instance, have their own bulletin boards to share information and offer mutual support.

E-mail

Finally, electronic mail can provide a sense of contact with friends and relatives during stressful times. Here's a personal example. A friend and I sent messages back and forth during a recent family crisis of hers. Although we often talked by phone, E-mail supplemented our conversation and allowed a somewhat different, more ruminative form of communication that helped us both. My friend, who had never dealt with the sort of problem she was facing, seemed to appreciate my support and sense of perspective. I found our exchange useful, too, since it clarified my thinking about one of my own experiences with loss. E-mail can be especially convenient, too, if you need to contact a number of people with the same message. For instance, you can send identical, simultaneous messages to any of your friends or relatives who are also on-line.

$\mathcal{F}$urther Reading

What follows isn't an exhaustive bibliography of books about loss; rather, it's a selection of books likely to be useful during or after a loss or other personal crisis. I've broken the list down into several categories. Inevitably, there's some overlap of subjects between them. I haven't listed the addresses for major publishers; you can locate them easily through any bookstore or in the Bowker publication *Books in Print*. However, I've indicated how to reach lesser-known publishers directly. Note, too, that many of the agencies listed in this appendix publish leaflets or books pertaining to one or more aspects of illness, death, and bereavement.

Loss and Bereavement (Including the Aftermath of a Death)

Ascher, Barbara L. *Landscape Without Gravity: A Memoir of Grief.* New York: Viking Penguin, 1994. A personal account of coping with grief.

Bernstein, Joanne E. *Loss.* New York: Clarion Books, 1977. Concise, clear advice on dealing with loss and bereavement.

Caine, Lynn. *Lifelines.* New York: Doubleday & Co., 1978. The problem of loneliness and how to overcome it.

Colgrove, Melba et al. *How to Survive the Loss of a Love.* Los Angeles: Prelude Press, 1991. Advice, meditations, and poems about dealing with grief.

Grollman, Earl, ed. *Concerning Death: A Practical Guide for the Living.* Boston: Beacon Press, 1974. Comprehensive guide to issues of death and loss.

———. *Living When a Loved One Has Died.* Boston: Beacon Press, 1974. Reassuring essays about coping with loss.

Henderson, Diane. *Coping with Grief.* Tuscumbia, AL: Henderson Clark Publishers, 1979. A short booklet about the grief process.

Kübler-Ross, Elisabeth. *Death: The Final Stage of Growth.* New York: Macmillan Publishing Co., 1981. Essays and photo-essays about the dying.

———. *Living with Death and Dying.* New York: Macmillan Publishing Co., 1981. Essays about various issues of death and dying.

———. *On Death and Dying.* New York: Macmillan Publishing Co., 1981. A classic, popular work about understanding death and dying.

Kushner, Harold S. *When Bad Things Happen to Good People.* New York: Avon Books, 1981. A rabbi's insights into coping with personal hardship and tragedy.

Levine, Stephen. *Healing into Life and Death.* New York: Doubleday, 1989. Insights into illness and death as transformative experiences.

———. *Who Dies?* New York: Anchor/Doubleday, 1989. Similar in nature to the author's book noted previously.

Lewis, C. S. *A Grief Observed.* New York: Bantam Books, 1983. A famous theologian's observations on loss and grief.

Manning, Doug. *Don't Take My Grief Away.* New York: Harper & Row, 1984. Recommendations similar to those offered in the book previous.

Miller, Jack. *Healing Our Losses: A Journal for Working Through Your Grief.* San Jose, CA: Resource Publishers, 1993. A workbook approach to resolving bereavement.

Moffat, Mary J., ed. *In the Midst of Winter: Selections from the Literature of Mourning.* New York: Random House, 1992. An anthology of writings about grief and bereavement.

Myers, Edward. *When Parents Die: A Guide for Adults,* revised ed. New York: Penguin Books, 1997. An exploration of the specific bereavement issues facing adults following a parent's death.

Rapoport, Nessa. *Woman's Book of Grieving.* New York: Morrow, 1994. Advice on bereavement specifically for women.

Sanders, Catherine. *Surviving Grief . . . and Learning to Live Again.* New York: John Wiley & Sons, Publishers, 1992. Recommendations for dealing with the grief process.

Tatelbaum, Judy. *The Courage to Grieve.* New York: Harper & Row, 1984. Useful recommendations about dealing with grief.

Temes, Roberta. *Living with an Empty Chair.* Amherst, MA: Mandala, 1977. An unusually eloquent commentary on loss and grief.

Vail, Elaine. *A Personal Guide to Living with Loss.* New York: John Wiley & Sons, 1982. Comprehensive treatment, including practical matters.

Viorst, Judith. *Necessary Losses.* New York: Ballantine Books, 1987. A writer's insights into loss and bereavement.

Volkan, Vamik, and Elizabeth Zintl. *Life After Loss: The Lessons of Grief.* New York: Macmillan, 1994. The nature and process of bereavement.

Scholarly Literature on Loss and Bereavement

Bowlby, John. *Attachment and Loss.* Vol. 1, *Attachment.* New York: Basic Books, 1980. A detailed study of human attachment behavior.

———. *Attachment and Loss.* Vol. 2, *Anxiety and Anger.* New York: Basic Books, 1980. The consequences of disrupted attachment in humans.

———. *Attachment and Loss.* Vol. 3, *Loss.* New York: Basic Books, 1980. A study of bereavement and loss.

Cook, Alicia S., and Daniel S. Cook. *Helping the Bereaved: Therapeutic Interventions for Children, Adolescents, and Adults.* New York: Basic Books, 1992. Recommendations for mental health professionals regarding bereavement.

Jacobs, Selby. *Pathologic Grief: Maladaptation to Loss.* Washington, DC: American Psychiatric, 1993. Technical overview of problematic bereavement reactions.

Leick, Nimi, and Marianne Davidsen-Nielsen. *Healing Pain: Attachment, Loss, and Grief Therapy.* New York: Routledge, 1991. An overview of bereavement and therapeutic intervention for the bereaved.

Lifton, Robert Jay. *The Life of the Self.* New York: Basic Books, 1983. Theoretical essays on life and death.

Margolis, Otto S. et al. *Acute Grief: Counseling the Bereaved.* New York: Columbia University Press, 1981. A wide range of essays on issues of acute grief.

Osterweis, Marion et al., eds. *Bereavement: Reactions, Consequences, and Care.* Washington, DC: National Academy Press, 1984. A compendium of articles about loss and grief.

Parkes, Colin Murray. *Bereavement: Studies of Grief in Adult Life.* New York: International Universities Press, 1977. An English psychiatrist's research on grief.

Parkes, Colin Murray, and Robert S. Weiss. *Recovery from Bereavement.* New York: Basic Books, 1983. A detailed study of widowhood in America and England.

Piper, William E. *Adaptation to Loss Through Short-Term Group Psychotherapy.* New York: Guilford Press, 1992. Information for mental health professionals regarding bereavement therapy.

Raphael, Beverley. *The Anatomy of Bereavement.* New York: Basic Books, 1983. A detailed, inclusive study of all aspects of loss.

Miscellaneous Topics (by Category)

Alcoholism and Other Addictions

Wegscheider, Sharon. *Another Chance: Hope and Health for Alcoholic Families*. Palo Alto, CA: Science and Behavior Books, 1981. Recommendations for relatives of alcoholics.

Divorce

Belli, Melvin, and Mel Krantzler, Ph.D. *Divorcing: The Complete Guide for Men and Women*. New York: St. Martin's Press, 1988. A lawyer's and psychologist's cowritten manual for dealing with divorce.

Fassel, Diane, Ph.D. *Growing Up Divorced: A Road to Healing for Adult Children of Divorce*. New York: Pocket Books, 1991. A psychologist's recommendations for coping with the aftermath of divorce.

Margolis, Sam. *Getting Divorced Without Ruining Your Life*. New York: Fireside, 1992. A guide to navigating the practical and emotional tasks of divorce.

Wallerstein, Judith S. *Second Chances*. New York: Ticknor & Fields, 1989. A study of divorce and its consequences.

Dreams

Taylor, Jeremy. *Dream Work: Techniques for Discovering the Creative Power in Dreams*. New York: Paulist Press, 1983.

Ullman, Montague, and Nan Zimmerman. *Working with Dreams*. New York: G. T. Putnam's Sons, 1979.

Practical Tasks

Bloomfield, Harold H. *Making Peace with Your Parents*. New York: Random House, 1983. A self-help manual for adults in conflict with their parents.

Silverstone, Barbara, and Helen Kandel Hyman. *You and Your Aging Parent*. New York: Pantheon, 1982. An excellent guidebook for helping and dealing with elderly parents.

Relationships, Including Marriage

Aroud, Miriam, and Samuel L. Pauker, M.D. *The First Year of Marriage.* New York: Warner, 1987. Advice for dealing with expectations, conflicts, and needs early in marriage.

Beattie, Melody. *Codependent No More.* New York: Harper & Row, 1987. A program for avoiding codependence with addictive personalities.

Botwin, Carol. *Men Who Can't Be Faithful.* New York: Warner, 1988. A guide for women coping with a husband's infidelity.

Bradshaw, John. *Bradshaw on the Family.* New York: Health Communications, Inc., 1993. A well-known psychologist's reflections on family dynamics.

————. *Creating Love.* New York: Bantam Books, 1993. Advice on keeping love alive in relationships.

Branden, Nathaniel. *The Psychology of Romantic Love.* New York: Bantam Books, 1980. Insights into love and relationships.

Carter, Betty, M.S.W., and Joan K. Peters. *Love, Honor and Negotiate: Making Your Marriage Work.* New York: Pocket, 1996. The importance of negotiation as a key to marital happiness.

Clephane, Ellen J., Ph.D. *Dance of Love: What Fifty Couples Say Makes Successful Relationships Really Work.* Rockport, MA: Element, 1995. A psychologist's recommendations for creative relationships.

Edell, Ronnie. *How to Save Your Marriage from an Affair: Seven Steps to Rebuilding a Broken Trust.* New York: Kensington, 1983. A program for coping with infidelity and its consequences.

Evans, Patricia. *The Verbally Abusive Relationship: How to Recognize It and How to Respond.* Holbrook, MA: Adams Media Corporation, 1996. Recommendations for coping with psychological abuse.

Gray, John, Ph.D. *Men, Women, and Relationships.* New York: Harper Spotlight, 1993. A bestselling author's advice for deepening love and commitment.

Halpern, Howard M., Ph.D. *How to Break Your Addiction to a Person.* New York: Bantam Books, 1982. A psychologist's advice on dealing with dependent relationships.

Harvey, John H. *Odyssey of the Heart: The Search for Closeness, Intimacy, and Love.* New York: W. H. Freeman & Company, 1995. Advice for establishing long-lasting relationships.

Kaufman, Taube S. *The Combined Family.* New York: Insight Books, 1993. An overview of and recommendations about blended families and the tasks of stepparenting.

Kipnis, Aaron, Ph.D., and Elizabeth Herron, M.A. *What Women and Men Really Want: Creating Deeper Understanding and Love in Our Relationships.* Novato, CA: Nataraj, 1995. Two psychologists' recommendations for building strong relationships.

Moore, Thomas. *Soul Mates: Honoring the Mysteries of Love and Relationships.* New York: HarperCollins, 1994. The psychology and spirituality of human relations.

Rosen, Margery D., and the editors of *Ladies Home Journal. Can This Marriage Be Saved?* New York: Workman, 1994. A compendium of articles on marital crises drawn from the well-known women's magazine.

Rountree, Cathleen. *The Heart of Marriage: Discovering the Secrets of Enduring Love.* New York: HarperCollins, 1996. The author's program for marital happiness.

Rubin, Lillian B. *Intimate Strangers: Men and Women Together.* New York: Harper & Row, 1983. The differences between men and women and how they affect relationships.

Sills, Judith, Ph.D. *Biting the Apple: Women Getting Wise About Love.* New York: Viking Press, 1996. A psychologist's program for "loving men more by needing them less."

Stearns, Ann Kaiser. *Living Through Personal Crisis.* New York: Ballantine Books, 1990. Advice for coping with adversity in relationships.

Wallerstein, Judith S., and Sandra Blakeslee. *The Good Marriage: How and Why Love Lasts.* Boston: Houghton Mifflin Company, 1995. A study of fifty American couples and why they find that their marriages are stable, loving, and intimate.

Suicide

Barrett, Terence. *Life After Suicide: A Survivor's Grief Experience.* Fargo, ND: Aftermath Research, 1989. A personal account of coping with the aftermath of suicide.

Grollman, Earl A. *Suicide: Prevention, Intervention, and Post-Intervention.* Boston: Beacon, 1988. Recommendations for dealing with suicide and its aftermath.

Hendin, Herbert. *Suicide in America.* New York: Norton, 1982. An overview of suicide among Americans.

Schneidman, Edwin S., and Norman L. Farberow. *Clues to Suicide.* New York: McGraw-Hill, 1957. A classic study of suicide.

Widowhood

American Association of Retired Persons. *On Being Alone.* Long Beach, Calif.: AARP Widowed Persons Service, 1984. Address: Box 199, Long Beach, CA 90801. A booklet about adjustment to widowhood.

Antoniak, Helen, et al. *Alone: Emotional, Legal and Financial Help for the Widowed or Divorced Woman.* Millbrae, CA: Les Femmes/Celestial Arts, 1979. Practical information for widows and divorcees.

Brothers, Joyce. *Widowed.* New York: Ballantine, 1992. Advice on dealing with widowhood.

Burges, Jane, and Willard Kohn. *The Widower.* Boston: Beacon Press, 1978. A practical guide for widowers.

Caine, Lynn. *Widow.* New York: Bantam, 1981. A first-person account of widowhood.

Fisher, Ida, and Byron Lane. *The Widow's Guide to Life.* Englewood Cliffs, NJ: Prentice-Hall, 1981. A comprehensive book for recent widows.

Loewinsohn, Ruth J. *Survival Handbook for Widows.* Chicago: Follett, 1979. Address: c/o New Century, 275 Old New Brunswick Road, Piscataway, NJ 08854. A concise guide for widows.

Shachter, Stephen R. *Dimensions of Grief: Adjusting to the Death of a Spouse.* San Francisco: Jossey Bass, 1986. An overview of widowhood and recommendations for coping with it.

Tawes, Isabella. *The Widow's Guide.* New York: Schocken Books, 1981. Discussions of practical and emotional aspects of widowhood.

Index